praise for
why can't we just play?

Why Can't We Just Play is smart, funny, insightful, and refreshingly honest. You'd think that Pam Lobley and I would be opposites—tiger mom vs. play mom—but I loved and totally related to her determination to parent against the tide. Entertaining and endearing, this book reminds us that parenting can be at once the most absurd, the most humbling, and the mostly deeply rewarding thing any of us ever do.

—AMY CHUA, Yale Law Professor and author of *Battle Hymn of the Tiger Mother* and *The Triple Package: How Three Unlikely Traits Explain the Rise and Fall of Cultural Groups in America*

When Pam Lobley came to the realization that the vision she had for her family life—lingering over books, laughing fits at bedtime—in no way resembled the panicked, exhausting mad rush of her days, she set out to re-create the 1950s. Literally. *Why Can't We Just Play?* is her touching, honest and amusing account of the summer she gave her kids the gift of boredom and set a goal for herself that was both simple and profound: to learn to pay attention to her life as she lived it.

—BRIGID SCHULTE, author of the NYT bestselling *Overwhelmed: Work, Love, and Play When No One Has the Time*

Pam Lobley is irresistibly funny and forthright, a breath of fresh air as she sounds off about the benefits (and downsides) of giving her two sons a summer with no obligations. Honest and clear-eyed, what sounds like every parent's dream—a summer of family time and fun—becomes a rollercoaster of the good, the bad and the ugly. All-in-all, a great comment on how we could all use 'time off' if only we can deal with the shock of an empty calendar, two energetic boys with no plans, and the social pressures of friends who are still living from activity-to-activity.

—MONICA HOLLOWAY, author of *Driving with Dead People,*
Cowboy & Wills, and the upcoming *There Goes Perfect*

why can't we just play?

FAMILIUS

Published by Familius LLC, www.familius.com

Familius books are available at special discounts for bulk purchases, whether for sales promotions or for family or corporate use. For more information, contact Familius Sales at 559-876-2170 or email orders@familius.com.

Library of Congress Cataloging-in-Publication Data
2015956716

Print ISBN 9781942934578
Ebook ISBN 9781942934967
Hardcover ISBN 9781942934974

Printed in the United States of America

Edited by Michele Robbins
Cover design by David Miles
Book design by Brooke Jorden

10 9 8 7 6 5 4 3 2 1

First Edition

why can't we just play?

WHAT I DID WHEN I REALIZED MY KIDS WERE WAY TOO BUSY

Pam Lobley

For my mom and dad, with love.

contents

introduction

I 'm standing in the kitchen wearing high heels and pearls cooking a Baked Alaska. It's August, and it's hot. It's hot in the kitchen, and it's hot outside. My husband is outside getting the grill ready for the steaks I bought, and I am inside running back and forth between the Baked Alaska and my beautifully set dining room table. I light the candles. I adjust the salad forks and tuck place cards into napkin rings. I stop in front of the mirror and check my lipstick.

We are in the middle of our 1950s summer, and this our 1950s dinner party.

The guests are arriving, and one couple has even dressed in 1950s style for the occasion. It is a very festive idea, this theme dinner, and we are all laughing a lot. I am really enjoying myself, although my feet are already starting to swell from standing around in front of a hot stove in pumps.

We eat the steaks, we try Spam kabobs, we have fun visiting another era. I got some recipes, set my hair, played some Perry Como music. It was a noisy, fun evening with an overlay of giddy period shtick.

The summer, though, was meant to be more than just fun. It was meant to be radically different. I had that *Stop the world, I want to get off* feeling and was trying to approach life differently. I wanted to give up being contemporary. Trying to keep up in today's dizzying world seemed to be the root of all our family stress. *Let's go back to a simpler time*, I thought, *and see who we can be then.*

My breakthrough 1950s idea was hatched the previous spring. At the time, my two boys were ages eight and ten, and life was busy. The pleasant slow days of naps and preschool and seven o'clock bedtime were well behind us, and we were smack in the middle of what my mother called *the golden age of childhood*—those years when a child is between five and twelve years old. It didn't feel golden, though. It felt rushed and blurred. We were *too* busy. Many of the reasons I had wanted children—lingering over books, laughing fits at bedtime, meandering days of outside play—never had time to happen, because all we did was steer ourselves through jam-packed days of homework, organized sports, and structured activities. It wasn't bad, really, and everyone I knew was doing the same thing, but I felt hollow. At the time, I wasn't working—that is to say, I was a freelance writer, which on most days meant I was simply unemployed. I was writing a bimonthly column in a local newspaper and working on a play. I wrote around the kids' schedules, and I was always there for them. So I was there, all day every day, and I still felt I was missing my children's childhood.

I constantly told myself *It will get better when soccer is over* or *It's just crazy now because of the holidays*, and I would wait for it to feel calmer. Of course, it never did. And then that spring, in the middle of a cold, rainy March, I started to think about summer.

I didn't think of it with longing; I was not daydreaming or musing, "Gee, I long for those hot and lazy days of summer." No, I was panicking. I was thinking, *Holy cow, I gotta make some plans for the kids this summer.* If you have kids, by March, you are either all set with your summer plans or starting to scramble about for what your children are going to DO during those ten weeks.

Yes, ten weeks. That's how long it is. "Summer" sounds quick, brief, fleeting. "Ten weeks" sounds more like what it really is: many, many days that need to be filled. And, in case you forgot, the days are really long. It does not get dark outside until ten o'clock. My kids wanted to be active until that time every night, and when they finally did come inside, their feet were black with dirt and they were sweaty and covered in bug spray, so they needed a good bath before bed. This bath did not soothe them or wind them down—it gave them a second wind. They would stay up giggling for hours.

I didn't want to think about summer plans; in fact, I didn't want to think about any plans. All I did was plan. Plan dinner, plan the play-date, plan the weekend activities, plan plan plan! I tried not to think about it, but I got the swim club dues in the mail and was forced to think about dates for swim lessons. This made me realize that I didn't know what camps, if any, my kids would do. Would they do swim team again? Tennis? At that point, I didn't even know what dates we were going away for vacation, so how could I pick which week they would do swim lessons? The pressure was building.

This is how the world operates: you buy your bathing suit in April, your back-to-school supplies in July, and your Halloween costume just after Labor Day. You take your Christmas photo on vacation, your Christmas decorations go up over Thanksgiving, and then you're free to bake your brains out for the cookie swap before falling into a stupor just before New Year's. Help me.

Looking for guidance, I started asking around among my friends. What were their kids doing for the summer? Most responded with rote speech: outdoor day camp, a week with Grandma, a super fun science camp where they get really messy . . . ugh. My friend Jane, though, obviously feeling the same frustration that I was, blurted out to me, "Nothing! We're having a summer from the 1950s!"

That stopped me in my tracks. A summer from the 1950s . . . what perfume . . . what seduction . . . what bliss. Moms didn't plan their children's lives in the 1950s; they just let them play. I swooned as I imagined my two boys, suddenly with crew cuts and tucked-in shirts, playing happily on the lawn or at the pool, easily filling their days with all manner of wholesome activities without the least bit of help or direction from me.

I saw my husband, also in a crew cut and tucked-in shirt, drive up the driveway at five thirty p.m. on the dot. I saw him get out of the car smiling, not the least bit stressed from work or traffic, roll up his sleeves, and toss a ball around with the kids. Then I saw myself in a smooth ponytail and tucked-in shirt, setting the picnic table with some checkered napkins and bringing out some juicy steaks for the grill. I saw my family eat a healthful and organized meal, the kids sitting up straight and speaking clearly and excitedly about their adventures in the tree house or how they caught a frog but then, kindly, let him go.

Could I really have a summer from the 1950s? Would the kids like it? Would it be hard? I knew I was fantasizing about a time that never truly existed; the 1950s had polio, segregated schools, and the McCarthy hearings. I knew that the wholesome, happy families of the 1950s were in many ways a myth. However, myths are powerful. They can inspire us to higher thinking and better ways of behavior. I didn't want to go to the real 1950s, but I sure did want to go to those mythical years. It's like when you watch reruns of the sitcom *Friends* and you know that no bunch of twenty-year-olds in New York City could ever afford an apartment like that but you don't care if it's real—you just want to believe.

I wanted to believe there was still a summer out there that could be free of pressure, where sports are played for fun, not on organized teams with four games a week. A summer where kids read books in the middle of the day for enjoyment, not because I'm making them read a certain number of chapters a week. A summer where kids get so bored they actually invent new stuff to do, or pick up a new hobby, or daydream. I wanted to do a little daydreaming myself.

I knew that what really happened in summer is that we all got on each other's nerves. That each day was a battleground on which I tried to keep the kids away from video games, TV, and the computer. I knew that the sibling bickering could get vicious as early as breakfast time and that many nights when my husband gets home from work, my first words to him would be "I NEED SOME TIME ALONE!"

My friend Jane had been kidding about the 1950s summer, but I couldn't let it go. I felt I was onto something and couldn't resist the urge. Which is how I came to be standing at the stove, testing the stiffness of my meringue while listening to "Papa Loves Mambo." The ambling and relaxed summer from the 1950s had beckoned. I didn't care if it was ever real. I just thought about summer and kids, and I wanted to believe.

can't we just talk
a little more?

Suddenly YOU make the decisions!

—Tampax ad, 1955

You can't devote every minute of every day of your life to the children. It isn't fair to them, and it isn't fair to us.

—Jim Anderson to his wife, Margaret,
Father Knows Best, "Second Honeymoon," 1954

Mrs. Lobley, I have your son Sam here. He has a fever of 102. Can you come pick him up?

—Mrs. Davis, the school nurse,
9:45 on a Wednesday morning

I 've always been someone who ignores the word "no." It's not that I'm obstinate by nature; it's just that I prefer the road not taken. When I want to do something, all the reasons why I can't don't make sense. I hear them, but I don't heed them. As my grandfather used to say, "Don't bother me with the facts—my mind is made up."

So completely chucking all the present-day parenting wisdom out the window and trying something different didn't seem that daunting. I had done tougher things. It was worth a try.

The truth was, I had been looking for something. I knew something was missing in our lives. I knew we were too busy all the time. I was so sick of the pace and pressure that dictated family life and the constant feeling that if you let up for one minute, your child will fall behind. That is the cardinal sin of parenting today in the middle class: letting your child fall behind.

I thought I was pretty good at keeping the pressure at bay. I prided myself on sensible parenting. For instance, we never rushed home from school to do homework. I let my kids play outside after school on the playground for up to an hour every day. The boys would burst out of the school at three o'clock, dump their backpacks at my feet, and dash off to the farthest reaches of the playground with their friends. This gave me the opportunity to stand around with like-minded moms and conjecture yet another fascinating way that we might serve chicken for dinner.

I had been very careful to say no to intensive athletic competitions, to extra homework, or to too many activities that might cut into their downtime. I was doing a good job at keeping the balance in our lives—or so I thought, until one Friday night the previous November, my son Sam, age ten, broke down in sobs at bedtime. "I never have time to just play!" he cried.

What?

As my little fifth grader gasped and moaned out his schedule, my heart sank: chorus, band, Musically Talented Group, safety patrol, Cub Scouts, soccer, and CCD every Sunday. I winced as I heard it out loud, but everything he was doing he had wanted to do. I didn't push him to do a thing. He just kept coming home with more and more sign-up sheets saying, "Mom, I want to do this!"

What I didn't realize was that he could not control his own appetite for activity, and our schools and community offered a large array of tantalizing choices. He was like an overeater at a buffet, not knowing when to stop.

He quit chorus that week, then soccer season ended, and I was careful to add nothing more. My younger son Jack was doing karate, attending two classes a week, and he was getting pressure to attend more so that he could progress faster. There were kids his age who were getting their black belts. Jack had his blue belt, which is about eight colors away from black. Then Jack wanted to try the wrestling team. They had five-hour matches on Saturday mornings. Soon, it was Jack's turn to cry.

Wrestling ended. Then it was spring. I waited for that feeling of relief to kick in. The feeling that things were calmer—we could relax. We could have fun.

But things weren't calmer for me or for my husband, Bill. Bill was working long hours and volunteering as a Cub and Boy Scout leader, and I was busy with writing projects and volunteering at church. I was a class mom. Field trip, anyone?

Must We Make It Special?

We all know that feeling—kids grow up so fast that you simply MUST enjoy every moment. So you sign up for class mom, and you bake the special cupcakes for the birthday snack, and you drag the video camera to every little recital. And you throw birthday parties and Halloween parties and you make special waffles on Saturday mornings. Let's make today special, let's savor this time. Well, I was so exhausted from making it special all the time that I was too tired to enjoy it. I was so busy creating moments to savor that I didn't have time to savor them. Nobody can enjoy every moment. People have been trying for centuries. It can't be done!

Somehow, though, in the age of the Internet and Botox and robots that vacuum, we feel we all can master our destinies in a way we never could before. Surely NOW we are capable of enjoying every moment, now that we have all this helpful technology. Even worse, we feel there is something wrong with us if we can't enjoy every moment. Everybody else is enjoying every moment, or at least they look like they are on Facebook, Pinterest, and Snapchat. Maybe the problem is me. Maybe I needed to meditate or to exercise more or to read the latest self-help book. Then I'd be able to enjoy every moment.

And then I began to read and research the 1950s. I got quite a dose of perspective. The 1950s were a time when people enjoyed *some* of the moments. They didn't expect too much. Their kids didn't fall behind; they just acted like kids. No eight-year-old had their black belt in the 1950s. Women didn't try to have fulfilling careers *and* a fulfilling motherhood. Heck, they didn't even try to have fulfilling motherhood—they just tried for regular motherhood. That was fulfilling enough. Fathers didn't race home from work to coach a bunch of ten-year-olds on a county-wide competitive basketball team. The kids shot hoops at the park until Dad came home and the family sat down to dinner together. That was enough. Enough was enough.

Now, too much is not enough. Because no matter how busy and accomplished you are, there is a family doing it better than you. Their kids play the piano at a concert level, they go to Johns Hopkins Brainy Kid Summer Camp, the mother makes all the window treatments in their house, and the dad drives a spotless Mercedes SUV. I avoid those families. They're nothing but trouble.

Our culture is obsessed with "having it all." Who has it all? It strikes me as a ridiculous concept: *all*. Would you go into a restaurant, look at the menu, and say, "I'll have it all"? Would you go into a furniture store, glance around at the various sofas and coffee tables, and declare, "I'll take it all"? Yet most of the focus of our adult lives involves trying to have it all. Suddenly, all I wanted was less: less striving, less achieving, less rushing. Certainly, my children were craving less. If that put us at odds with contemporary values, it seemed to line right up with those of the 1950s. I knew we needed to take the plunge and try a 1950s, old-fashioned summer.

What Is Abundance, Anyway?

I told my mother about my no-plans summer, and I told my mother-in-law, too. They both seemed nonplussed. It was as if they were thinking, "Duh, it's summer. Of course you're doing nothing."

My mother looks at me and thinks, *Why is she doing so much?* And I think, *Am I supposed to be this tired?*

My generation feels empowered and energized—the world is our oyster. We work hard, we expect to achieve, and we DO achieve. Boy, do we achieve. We're so busy achieving that we barely sleep six hours a night.

We're not just doing more; we're doing it better. This is because everywhere you look, there are helpful magazines, websites, cable channels, and books that show you how to be the best you can be.

You can now excel at everything. You can have a prettier patio, six-pack abs, a fresh-scented sofa, a high-performing retirement fund, a meaningful marriage, a dry basement, well-behaved children, and robust gum health. In fact, if you don't have all these things, it's your own darn fault. You're probably just lazy. Don't you *want* to be better?

The irony is that with all the unprecedented ways in which an average person can go, do, and acquire, we don't feel happy and satisfied. We feel panicked and grabby. There are so many choices that you can't escape the feeling that you're missing something.

In the 1950s, Americans had a feeling of limitless possibility. After the Depression and World War II, they had peace and prosperity. They had been through two decades of fear and sacrifice and loss. They knew a good thing when they saw it. They could buy a car and a TV and a house. They could expect that their kids would go to college. Of course they worked hard at their jobs, as they always had, but there was a future, and it was bright. Abundance was theirs.

We don't feel abundant today. Every time we turn around, we see that America is not the best anymore: our jobs are being lost overseas; our kids are being out-schooled by third-world countries. Our struggling economy has us competitive and nervous. To make ourselves feel better, we crave bigger TVs, bigger cars, and bigger houses. We need enormous kitchens with six-burner stoves. Who is doing all this cooking that they need SIX burners? When was the last time you had all four burners going and thought, "Darn it, if I just had two more burners, I could REALLY cook a good meal!"

What Do Our Kids Need?

We cannot escape the fear that our children will fall behind because it is fed to us daily through the newspapers, magazines, and TV shows. We have all accepted it as a fact that a good college is nearly impossible to get into and that our kids have almost no chance of getting there unless they have perfect grades and high SAT scores and play at least one sport or musical instrument at a recruitable level. And if the kids can't handle that much work or that much pressure or if they become antsy or angry or depressed, then maybe they need some medication, too, just to help them grow up and handle it all.

Even though I had been trying so hard to stay out of the parenting rat race, I had to admit it: I got sucked in. So I tried slowing down, cutting back, and simplifying. All the things the magazines tell you to do. I tried to squeeze in a few board games or movie nights, we went bowling, I taught them charades. It was fun.

One night in early spring, I was tucking Sam and Jack into their cozy beds. It had been a typical day of yelling, fighting between siblings, slogging through homework, groaning through the dinner menu, and sloshing through the bath. Now they were relaxed. We said our prayers and snuggled and talked about little things I can't remember. Then I got up to go.

I still had a kitchen full of dinner dishes to do, and I hadn't even asked my husband about his day yet. I was anxious to get downstairs and watch a little TV. But Sam hugged me tightly as I tried to leave. "Can't we just talk a little more?" he asked.

I can remember my own mother having talking time with me at bedtime and how we would giggle and hug. It was such a sweet, special time. But the cozy closeness takes on real importance when the kids ask me what I think heaven looks like, or they tell me a friend was mean to them, or they mention they might want to be a teacher when they grow up, or they ask why we can't just buy a new car any time we want. Those conversations deserve real attention.

The talking then is easy because I'm not doing anything else. Normally, whenever I was talking with my kids, we were walking to school, or we were driving to errands, or they were supposed to be making their beds, or I was rushing them through chores. It wasn't really about the conversation. It was about getting through the day.

But they loved when we had conversations. When I paid attention to them and did nothing else. That was why bedtime could take so long: because we finally slowed down and paid attention to each other.

Now, here was Sam, his skinny arms clawing me, clamoring for connection. For that sweet, solid feeling of belonging and contentment you get when you spend time with family. All the charades and the movie nights weren't enough. They still craved more family time.

"Tell us a story about you and Aunt Virginia!" said Jack. From the other bed, he totally perked up at the idea of bedtime conversations. "Tell when she wet the bed and peed on Fluffy!"

Enjoy every moment! my subconscious whispered. And so I sat back down and let them hug and climb on me. And I told them about how Aunt Virginia peed on Fluffy and how Grammy had to wash him out and hang him by his ears to dry. I told them how I used to walk on stilts and was good at roller-skating and how our brother learned to tie a noose in Boy Scouts and hung all our dolls by their necks like common criminals.

They didn't want it to end, but I stopped after several stories. It was getting late, after all. I was struck by how they blossomed under these stories, how they delighted in my full attention. They were utterly happy, and we all belonged completely to each other. Why wasn't I making time for this every day?

Because I was too crabby and stressed out to make time for it every day, that's why! Although I told myself I was savoring moments, I was really just wildly creating them so I could say that I did it, hoping that the kids were at least savoring things while I just dashed madly about.

I had turned into a mom who didn't look up from her dishes or paperwork to answer her kids' questions. I was a mom who just slid the piles of homework, mail, and newspapers over to one side of the dining room table while we huddled at the other end eating dinner. I was a mom who let the kids eat in the car to save time while we did errands and then left messes of Cheez-It crumbs and empty water bottles in the backseat. Pretty soon, the car was like a garbage dump, and the kids didn't even notice it. They were used to it. Everything we did felt rushed and second rate.

What Kind of a Mother Am I?

On a Saturday afternoon in late May, I took Sam to a birthday party. The party was for good friends of his, boy-girl twins, and it was in their backyard. They were going to turn on the sprinkler, and there was a Slip'N Slide, and all of his friends would be there. He had talked about it all week. I pulled up to the house at the appointed time: four o'clock p.m. Sam started to get out of the car. Then I saw kids with wet hair and towels leaving the house. They were laughing and carrying goody bags. The party was over.

I had messed up the time! I thought the party was from four to six o'clock, but it was from two to four o'clock. I hadn't even bothered to check the invitation again that morning. Sam, confused, cried out, "The party's over?" I burst into tears.

Not only was I driving a garbage dump of a car, and checking email when I should be making dinner, and forgetting to teach Jack, who was in the second grade, how to tie his own shoes; I couldn't even get my kid to a favorite birthday party.

What kind of a mother was I turning into? Would I be that mother who was always so frantic that their kid was always the last one picked up, standing in the rain alone, wondering where she was? Would I be too engrossed in a cell phone conversation to see Jack dart into a busy street to chase a ball? Would I be too distracted to take the time to talk to my children often about drugs, sex, self-esteem, and safe driving habits? Wasn't I already having trouble listening to them because my head was always someplace else?

We needed something drastic. We needed a total break from the present, a return to a simpler time. We needed a summer from the 1950s, and I vowed we were going to have it.

the grass is always greener over here

"Morning-Bath Freshness" lasts all day long! New "Protective Circle" checks underarm moisture 24 hours!

—Odo-Ro-No Deodorant ad, 1955

You know, I always thought being married would be pretty dull. But after spending an evening in this house, I've changed my mind.

—Tom, a guest,
Father Knows Best, "Matchmaker," 1955

Mom, your breath smells bad.

—My son Sam
when I kiss him good-bye before school

The kids were thrilled to be doing nothing all summer. They couldn't believe it. They brought home sign-up sheets in their backpacks for swim team, recreation camp, night camp, multi-sports camp, basketball camp, art classes, and nature camp. It became a game. I would hold up the sheet: "Anybody want to do soccer camp?" "NO!" they would chorus. "OK," I'd say and toss the paper in the trash. They'd grin like they were getting away with something. They couldn't wait to have nothing to do.

When I told other mothers what I was doing, their smiling faces froze. They tried to be polite, but I know they thought I was crazy. They would never, EVER consider letting their children be idle for so long. This is either because they work full time and need to put their kids in a program, because they want their kids to be as enriched and advanced as possible and are using the summer months to improve the sports or music skills of their children, or because, like most mothers with any common sense, they know if they just let their kids hang around the house all day, they, the parents, will lose their minds.

Some kids need an activity; they just can't entertain themselves. Mine, however, were always excellent at entertaining themselves. They stuffed wads of paper up their nose, beat each other with swords and lightsabers, zipped around without a helmet on Heelys, climbed over fences and up into trees, and burned their fingers on the dry ice that gets delivered with Omaha steaks. At various times in their lives, I had stopped them from licking a sharp knife, putting plastic bags over their heads, playing in a car trunk, and tying stuff around their necks. Jack had his arms in three different casts before he was four years old. One Sunday morning when he was six, he was playing outside after church and fell on his head, and the next thing I know, he was strapped to a board in an ambulance on his way to a CT scan. (Thankfully, he was fine.)

When we went anywhere in public, they always got the most out of the trip. At ages two and four, strapped into a double stroller and wheeling through the mall, they would poke, squeeze, and swat at each other, laughing and shouting insults at each other in their own invented language. "LEE SAR SAY! LEE SAR SAY!" I would see other adults looking at me with pity. "That poor woman," they were thinking. "She has not one but two mentally challenged children."

At the ages of three and five, they would readily accompany me to any public women's restroom, where they would crawl around on the floor and peek under the stalls, startling old ladies. At the ages of four and six, they could perk up any trip to CVS by shouting "Itchy butt crack!" at each other while standing in the checkout line. On a shopping trip to Kohl's, Sam, then age ten, jumped up onto a display to pose with the mannequin. He touched her hand, it fell off, and he laughed so hard he sprayed saliva.

So you see, there was no need to plan anything to keep them occupied. Unless, of course, I wanted sanity.

Thank goodness for TV. You're not supposed to use TV as a babysitter, but I always have done so, and so has every other mother I know—and the "experts" can stick it. In the 1950s, when the kids got too wild, the mom would tell her kids, "Get outside and have fun. I'll see you later."

Then the kids would go outside and play, and the mom would put on a dress, wax the floor, and whip up some Jell-O. Everyone would avoid getting on each other's nerves for most of the day.

But those days of drifting aimlessly from backyard to backyard— riding bikes, climbing trees, finding a dead bird, getting a drink from a hose—are long over. What made childhood so childlike was the combined freedom (roaming the neighborhood doing whatever) and safety (plenty of moms at home to supply a snack or a Band-Aid). This was the main problem with trying to have a summer from the 1950s: it wasn't the 1950s.

The social structure that allowed that kind of childhood had ceased to exist.

I couldn't give them the exact 1950s, but I could take what was free and wonderful about that decade and transpose it into something they could enjoy. I could remove all the dashing about and give them long, empty days to fill themselves. I could allow them to be bored without worrying if they were wasting time. They could fiddle with stuff. They could tinker. They could go outside and goof around on the lawn. Perhaps I could even reduce my own stress enough so that I would be able to listen to them when they talked.

My ace in the hole was our local town pool—a place where freedom and safety still coexist. The grounds are fenced in, so once you pass through those gates, your child is free to roam. There is no such thing as a playdate; it's just a bunch of kids running around, some you know and some you don't.

There are lots of moms and dads floating around keeping an eye—but not too close an eye—on the kids. The kids are as free as any child can be in this day and age. Of course, when they're in the pool, I watch them—but I don't have to play with them. And when they're not swimming, they're on the playground, playing Nok Hockey or checkers, climbing a tree, getting a baseball game going on the grass, playing cards, having a snack, or standing around in a posse sharing a joke with a curse word in it.

They are free to argue with other kids, free to bully or be bullied, without mothers constantly interfering and admonishing them to be nice, to share, to calm down. Free to make up their own games such as Walking Tag, Fast and Slow, and Ponytail Toss. Free to make their own mistakes and figure things out for themselves.

So I was planning on going to the pool every day, or almost every day. Other days, I figured we would have a friend over or maybe go to the movies, or they could just be stuck at home with their imaginations.

Turf Wars

My husband, Bill, was thrilled with my 1950s idea. This is a man who adores throwing theme parties, so to him, a 1950s summer is one long event. Will I get a bouffant? Can the kids get a BB gun? Should he shop for a cardigan?

Bill wears vintage bowling shirts, sings doo wop music in the shower, and has a Weber grill he darn near worships. He loves that grill. He loves his patio. And he loves his lawn. I mean, he REALLY loves his lawn.

Before we had kids, Bill and I lived in New York City in a studio apartment. We adored city living and New York. But we wanted a house and a yard to raise a family in, and when I got pregnant, we moved to New Jersey.

Since the whole time Bill and I had known each other we had been city dwellers, I had no way of knowing that I had married someone who would, one day, be obsessed with his lawn.

We bought a house on a small lot, 100 by 50 feet. During the first few years we lived there, Bill transformed our yard into an emerald gleaming in the sun. He weeded and aerated and mowed and limed and fertilized and de-grubbed and probably sang the grass a few love songs when he thought no one was listening. He watered—oh, did he water. Our water bill tripled every summer.

At first, I thought this was a charming and undeniably beneficial obsession. After all, we had the best-looking grass on the block, and we didn't even have a landscaping service. But things started to get tricky when our oldest, Sam, started walking. Bill didn't really want anyone walking on his lawn. Even his own one-year-old.

We certainly never installed any swing set or playground in the backyard—that would have just killed the grass. If we wanted to swing or climb, we went to the park. Like most toddlers, Sam loved to be chased, and I would chase him all over the lawn. Then Bill would come home, look at the grass, and say tensely, "Did you guys play outside today?"

Of course, he knew the answer. He could see our tracks in the matted grass. And he would go outside to set up the sprinkler and fluff up the grass again, checking for any divots or other damage that our delightful mother-and-son frolicking had caused.

Then we had another son, Jack, who also liked to be chased. And the boys liked to kick soccer balls and play croquet and pitch baseballs and run the bases. They liked fighting with swords and lightsabers. They had friends, lots of friends, who liked to come over and do those things, too.

If you have a beautiful green lawn that you would like to destroy, I have some ideas for you. You could invite four or five boys over, preferably after a day of rainfall when the earth is soft, and let them run all over the lawn in their sneakers, chasing, swordfighting, or kicking soccer balls. If you're lucky, they will fall and skid, tearing up several feet of turf in a single move.

You can turn on the sprinkler in the middle of the lawn and let several five-year-olds run back and forth in it over and over again in the very same spot until they have worn a dirt path and created a giant puddle in the grass.

You can leave the domed top to your plastic turtle sandbox on the grass on the summer's hottest day. The plastic dome will act like a microwave for your grass and burn a brown hole in your lawn in a mere matter of hours. The hole will be a perfect circle, exactly the shape of the turtle top, and it will take your husband three weeks to regrow the area to his satisfaction.

These are foolproof methods, believe me. I didn't do them on purpose; they happened in the normal course of family life, and Bill was upset, and then I would get upset with him for getting upset, because the real purpose of a lawn is to play on it, especially if you have kids. Bill disagrees and believes, instead, that the real purpose of a lawn is to look good and bring pride to the owner.

When I picture a 1950s summer, I always see happy kids on a nice, green lawn. Bill agrees, as long as it is not his lawn.

The 1950s Woman

So right off the bat, I had two challenges in my 1950s summer: my boys are crazy and the crazy boys will want to go on the lawn. And then there was this question—if a summer from the 1950s means unfettered fun for the kids, what does it mean for the mom? What did those '50s moms do while their kids played all day?

I am pretty sure I know. They cleaned house. They prepared wholesome meals. They went to Tupperware parties.

There has to be more than that, right? Many of those women did work, but the majority of mothers stayed home to care for the house and family. That sounds so easy compared to the pressures of today. Your husband went to work, your kids played outside with very little supervision by you, so you were free all day. Were they happier?

Magically, our local Friends of the Library was having a special program called "A 1950s Wedding," which is just what I needed to help me figure out what moms did back then.

As it turned out, the program was not really about weddings. It was about the lives of women in the 1950s in general. I couldn't wait to hear about it.

The woman running the program had been a 1950s housewife. She told us all about it: The search for a husband began right after high school and became increasingly urgent as you aged. She talked about what it was like to be twenty years old and feel the pressure to get married. There were very narrow definitions of what it meant to be a lady, and you did not veer from those parameters.

Once you got engaged, there was a whole stream of parties and gifts—teas, luncheons, showers. This is how you got the stuff you needed to start life as a housewife, and believe me, you needed stuff. She had several tables' worth of '50s artifacts laid out: chafing dishes, a wedding dress, a bed jacket, embroidered napkins and tablecloths, kitschy salt and pepper shakers, silver serving bowls, sheets that needed ironing, and tea sets. They needed tea sets because they were constantly having each other over for tea or coffee or dessert or lunch.

They waxed their kitchen floors; they polished their silver; they cooked everything from scratch every day. They wore dresses to do all this, with hose that were attached by garter belts and girdles. The '50s doesn't seem that long ago, but really, in terms of household inventions, it is way in the past. No wonder the kids were left on their own; the moms were worn out by housekeeping and stifled by their girdles. I felt claustrophobic just hearing about it.

I'd like to say that we modern women don't hold ourselves to the rigorous and unattainable housework standards of the 1950s, but that isn't true. Martha Stewart and Rachael Ray and leagues of other domestic gurus keep reminding us of the charm and desirability of a lovely home, delicious food, and delightful gardens. We want these things, and we feel compelled to work for them. We feel we should have these things even if we have demanding careers. We cut ourselves no slack. No matter how successful you are in the working world, if your home is a mess, you're flunking womanhood.

After the program, I felt deflated. I don't know what I was expecting—maybe to hear a few ways that I could have some 1950s-esque fun, but instead, it was just a litany of cleaning chores. I didn't think a return to floor waxing and molded casseroles was going to reduce my stress—quite the opposite. All those 1950s moms stayed home and "fulfilled" themselves with housewifery, and we know how that turned out. By the 1960s, they were either getting divorced or bingeing on afternoon soap operas. I certainly didn't want to go down that road.

Plus, listening to all that made me realize how little time I actually spend cleaning my house.

Moment of Personal Clarity: I'm a Slob

It's not that I hate housework; it's that I don't prioritize it. Reading, going to the pool, fixing dinner, playing with my kids, and writing this book are all way more important to me than any type of cleaning or dusting.

So I kept choosing to do something else over cleaning, and pretty soon the house looked like "who did it and ran." But the 1950s housewives found housework tremendously important: it defined them. It dawned on me that I should probably ramp up my cleaning to have a true '50s experience. Ugh.

My husband (theme-party man) thought I should throw out the video games, unplug the TV, and give the boys crew cuts. He wanted to see what would happen if they had nothing to play with but Lincoln Logs and a chemistry set. He was serious about these things, and I could tell he was frustrated and disappointed that I was not making this into some sort of gimmicky reality show. He actually suggested that we stop using the microwave. He was missing my point.

I think he was perceiving this whole thing as a romp, a fun summer project. We could create a spectacle of Tinker Toys in the living room and have picnics outside on red checkered tablecloths—something that we could photograph and blog about. But that would be more work than living the way we live normally. I was trying to do less, not more. To frantically create some sort of tableau and force my kids into all sorts of unnatural behavior (chemistry set?) would lead to MORE stress. Putting the emphasis on externals like clothing or cooking styles would lead to MORE detachment from each other. What I desperately craved was LESS. Less activity, less to supervise, less to live up to.

So I realized that it was up to me to make it up as I went along. That was intimidating, and I suddenly understood why parents get caught up in conformity. It's easier to just go with the flow than to question it and have to come up with something else.

But I had tried the flow, and it made me miserable. So miserable, in fact, that I was ready to try the 1950s even if I didn't really know what that was going to mean. I didn't want to turn this summer into some sort of theme-show project; I simply wanted to let the kids be free. It felt weird to have nothing planned for the next week, or the next month, or the month after that. It felt irresponsible, like I wasn't doing my job. Would they really like it? Would I really like it?

As I faced those yawning, empty days that summer, there was one thing about those 1950s housewives that I embraced: the care they took with their homes and meals, the way they broke out the china and silver for every occasion. This made me think that they were more concerned about celebrating the current moment as opposed to getting ahead to the next moment. This was the mindset I was looking for. I just wanted to be relaxed enough to unwrap the fun of each day.

school's out for summer

Should we cut down on meat during the hot weather months? Nutritionists tell us the answer is NO!

—American Meat Institute ad, 1952

Come 'n' get it! The steaks are ready, and are they mellow!

—Bud,
Father Knows Best, "Margaret Goes Dancing," 1954

Mom, can I put sugar on my hamburger?

—Jack, experimenting

Day One

Our first day of summer vacation was great. We slept in; I gave the dog a nice long walk. Sam and Jack stayed in their PJs until we got our bathing suits on to go to the pool around eleven a.m. As I mentioned, I was really counting on the pool. And the minute we got there, Sam sighed and announced that he was bored and the pool was stupid.

Twenty minutes later, Sam was having fun in the stupid pool with his boring friends. Thank goodness. Jack had found some friends, I spotted some of my favorite moms, and I just knew that summer was going to be fabulous. I felt the delicious pleasure of ten pressure-free weeks stretching out before me.

After a couple of hours, thunder sounded and they closed the pool. We went home and some friends came over, but they only stayed an hour because they had a baseball practice. So they left, and Sam was bored again. Was it too late to sign up for camp? Could we go buy a Lego? A new video game?

I knew they would be bored and whiny, but I didn't think it would happen in the first twenty-four hours. I suggested that we all have a quiet reading time, like for a half an hour, and the boys howled like I'd stuck them. So I let them turn on the TV, and I read, and then I fell asleep in the chair, and then I woke myself with my own loud snoring. Nice.

After the thunderstorm, Sam went outside and invented a new game: Awning Ball. He batted the Wiffle ball onto the awning over our patio, let it roll down, and then batted it up again. I felt triumphant. The first day of vacation and already his boredom was showing dividends. He was so resourceful! He was so creative! Of course, he kept running back and forth in the same spot and would most likely wear a path in the grass, causing his father to burst a vein, but never mind; he was entertaining himself in a wholesome summertime manner.

Bill came home and wanted to make a special first-day-of-vacation dinner on the grill. I normally would have said no to this because Bill takes three hours to prepare any meal, but since it was vacation and I was trying to be more relaxed, I said OK. We ate dinner at half past eight. After we ate, the kids played Awning Ball. Bill didn't notice the grass thing. It felt like the 1950s. I had a glowing sense of satisfaction.

It had been a great first day of summer. We didn't rush; we played outside; we dealt with boredom; we dealt with thunderstorms; we enjoyed each other's company; we ate healthy food; we didn't care what time it was. Terrific.

Just seventy-three days of summer left to go.

Day Two

My plan was to get my writing done in the morning and then have the rest of the day free to be the perfect 1950s mom. How telling is that? Though I was committed to being a '50s housewife, it still did not occur to me to give up working, even for a couple of months. Like many of the women in my generation, I define myself by my profession. This is understandable when you are a doctor, or a teacher, or a businesswoman that makes a good salary. But what if you're a humor columnist for a local newspaper with a paycheck that doesn't even cover the grocery bill? Wasn't I actually a SAHM with a hobby, not a career woman? Yes. Ouch, but yes.

Probably many writers have felt like this at times—that their career was really more of a hobby. In any case, I love my kids more than my career and always will, but that doesn't mean I didn't want that career. I had been working continually since having the boys, but mostly on projects that made little or no money. My daily focus had been on the children, but I was ready now to devote more time and energy to writing and make some real money. We needed the money, as all families do, and I needed to get some positive reinforcement in the form of cash. Giving my children some independence seemed like the right way to get more time for myself. And now I had convinced myself that going back to the 1950s would actually free me up to focus on my writing.

You see, normally my day was a choppy mess of shuffling kids, making meals, "quick" phone calls, last-minute errands, laundry, and trips to the gym to try to stave off middle-age flab. Before I knew it, it would be dinner time and I would have barely written two pages. I don't think this was how Hemingway got it done.

But, I told myself, this summer would be different. I wouldn't be flying around in all directions and driving kids to swim team practice or making lunches or picking kids up from camp. I would be able to finish a book and a play and easily produce my bimonthly newspaper columns.

Self-delusion—thy name is Mommy! What lies we tell ourselves so that we think we can do it all. Needless to say, my writing goals eventually clashed with my 1950s goals and caused a depressing emotional reckoning in August. But in the beginning of the summer, I was blissfully ignorant and had convinced myself that I would be a terrific 1950s mother *and* break new ground in my career.

While I was ascending to literary greatness in the morning hours, the kids played and watched TV. At some point, they would take out blocks and Legos and start building, all over the living room floor. They created exquisitely detailed structures: prisons, space stations, rockets, boxing rings with trapdoors. By ten a.m., you couldn't even walk through my living room, but who cared . . . my children were engineering geniuses!

One morning, I was sitting at my desk and Jack came up to give me a little Lego spaceship he had built himself. He had put it together out of spare parts, and it had three different shooters, a place to hold the captured bad guy, and a little section that detached and acted as a jetpack. He made it just for me and was so proud of it. I gave him a big hug and praised all its features two times then set it on my desk and got back to work. A few minutes later, he came back in and said, "Um, Mom? You know that spaceship I just gave you? Could I play with it for a while?"

By late morning, the bickering would start. The boys would get bored with TV and bored with building, and they would decide to spice things up by picking on each other. That's how I knew it was time to stop writing. I didn't have a set time to write each day—I just worked until the fighting got loud.

I summoned the energy to go through their school backpacks, which were loaded down with the year's detritus. I threw away mountains of stuff—worksheets, drawings, graded tests, colorful projects. It felt good, like a purge, and sad, like a farewell. My gosh, the year went fast. I felt a rush of relief that they were with me all day this summer. It made me feel like they were not growing up too quickly.

I tried to keep this feeling of warmth and closeness when I loaded them into the car to take them with me on errands. Banishing thoughts of "LEE SAR SAY" and "itchy butt crack," I tried to envision us having a pleasant, productive time as we accomplished small life tasks and spent unhurried time together. The whole point of this summer was for me to take a new approach to parenting. Taken from this vantage point, errands aren't a roster of chores that we have to finish before we can do something fun together—they ARE the something fun we can do together.

Our first fun errand of the summer was getting the dog vaccinated. Of course, the kids didn't want to do this because it meant turning off the TV. But then they realized that watching someone else get a shot might be kind of cool, so we all piled into the car.

Our dog, Oliver, was almost a perfect dog. A poodle/terrier mutt from a shelter, he was extremely affectionate, great with kids and other dogs, and never chewed on anything. He was thoroughly devoted to me. I swear he knew I spent months searching for him on Petfinder.com and hours of marital upheaval convincing Bill that we should get a dog.

We all wanted a dog in the worst way, except Bill. Bill did not want a dog. He knew that once we got a dog, his lawn would be under siege. Forever.

We got the dog, and we all loved him, even Bill. We just had to adapt. We fenced the yard, and we let Oliver out freely, but only during the winter months when the grass was dormant anyway. I would walk him a couple of times a day to make sure that most of his business was done around the neighborhood, not on our lawn. Once the spring came, it got trickier. During the growing months, April to October, Oliver was not supposed to be unsupervised on the lawn. If we were all outside having a cookout, or playing, and the dog wandered over to the grass to pee, our family went to DEFCON 2.

First, someone would shout the alert that the dog was sniffing, circling, and would most likely squat at any second. All activity would come to a halt. Someone would run and stand near Oliver and mark the spot. Someone else would retrieve the large bucket of water, which we always have at the ready, to pour over the spot and soak it, thereby hopefully minimizing the damage. If, by some hideous mistake, the bucket was not at the ready, someone would drag the hose out from the patio, shoving innocent dinner guests out of the way as the muddy hose flopped across the grass to the offending area, then another person would turn on the water—"TURN IT ON NOW!"—and saturate the area.

Occasionally, Oliver would squat a long time, his little eyes half closed in a super-relaxed fashion, as he was having an extra-long and really satisfying pee. No amount of water or quick action could save the spot in those cases.

When the dust settled after the watering, we returned to DEFCON 5: Watchful Waiting. Then we would conduct a series of postmortem repercussions like why wasn't the bucket filled (IT SHOULD ALWAYS BE FILLED), who didn't walk the dog earlier like they should have so that he wouldn't have had such a full bladder, is the dog drinking too much water, etc. Then Bill would huff a sigh, because nobody appreciated how hard he worked to keep the lawn nice, and refresh his drink, and the dog would find a nice comfy spot to lie down.

To be a part of our family means to live in deference to the lawn, and Oliver coped well with that. Like I said, he was almost a perfect dog, except for one thing. He threw up in the car.

We'd tried everything to help him stop puking. We thought it was just nerves and he'd get past it. He didn't. We tried Dramamine. Didn't work. The only thing that worked was a tranquilizer, which we would use when we drove someplace that took a long time, like on vacation. Other than that, we packed paper towels.

The vet was the maximum distance the dog could handle before he puked. A short drive to the park was no problem, and the few blocks to the groomer was OK, too. But the vet was a borderline situation, and we all hoped for light traffic.

Having the kids along with me when the dog threw up didn't really help the situation. Rather than holding the dog or handing me a paper towel, they would just shriek and provide color commentary. "Ewww, it looks just like his breakfast!" "It smells disgusting!" "He's going to eat it!"

The traffic on this day was light, and we got to the vet just fine. The kids were very helpful and fun to have along. On the way home, we spotted a nice, modern-looking desk at a neighbor's curb. It had been set out for trash, but it was in perfect condition. Taking other people's trash is a major suburban sport; if it doesn't sound fun to you, then you haven't tried it. I pulled over and told Sam we were taking the desk. He loved the idea. It felt like stealing, even though it wasn't, and that appealed to him.

We sweated and tugged and hoisted and finally got the thing into the back of the minivan. The desk was absurdly heavy, and I could never have done this by myself. I reminded myself that if Sam were in day camp right then, I would not have been able to get this desk. Having a 1950s summer was really paying off.

The desk didn't fit in the trunk, so we lowered the third row of seats, and then it still didn't fit, so we lowered the second row, which meant Jack had to sit on the floor next to the dog. We slammed the doors and drove off. The dog puked.

"Gross!" Jack screamed. "It looks like egg yolks!" "Grab his collar," commanded Sam, "before he tries to eat it again." "It's dripping off his chin!" wailed Jack.

I was right! Errands *are* something fun we can do together!

At home, Sam helped me drag the desk out of the car and up the driveway. Then he and Jack went inside. I cleaned up the dog. I cleaned up the dog puke. I washed off the desk, sweating profusely and getting sloppy water all over my clothes. The kids were relaxing inside watching TV. I stopped. Why was I busting my rear end out here while they simply relaxed in air-conditioned comfort?

Disturbing Realization: My Kids Are Lazy Bums Because I Allow Them to Be

I am embarrassed to admit that my husband and I weren't making our kids do chores. At the ages of eight and ten, they had never so much as emptied a wastebasket. Sure, they made their beds. They cleaned up, sort of, when we told them to. But all year long, we rushed around so much and they were so busy with homework and activities that it seemed counterproductive to make them do chores, too. For instance, often Sam would not be done with homework until eight thirty, and he still needed to shower and get to bed. Was I going to make him stay up later to fold his laundry? No. Watching him fold/stuff his T-shirts into a drawer at nine p.m. when I could have just tucked him into bed and then retreated downstairs to watch television would be more of a sacrifice than I could handle. I wanted him to go to bed!

On weekends, my husband and I would mow, weed, tidy, mop, launder, and polish while the kids watched hours of TV or played with friends. We let them watch all that TV because it kept them out of our hair while we were cleaning. Sam and Jack certainly could have done chores if we had simply made it a part of our routine. But Bill never wanted the boys to help in the yard because they wouldn't do it the way he likes it, and he couldn't stand that. I didn't make them dust or vacuum because I did it better and faster than they could.

The obvious answer to these problems would have been to simply *teach them* to do it the right way. Mmmhmm.

A few months earlier, I had tried to teach Sam how to do laundry. We stood in front of the washing machine while I explained about the knobs . . . cold water, hot water, etc. He nodded as if he understood. I went on to discuss soap, and he started fiddling with all the pens and coins on top of the dryer. He used a pen to draw something on his hand. I took the pen away and began explaining about dark and light colors. He put a Bounce sheet over his face and said, "Mmm, this smells like my clothes . . ." I pointed out that yes, it did, because those sheets go in the dryer with your clothes, but first we have to wash them. I turned on the water to fill the machine. He leaned into the washer, intrigued by the flat stream of water gushing forth. He stuck his hand in it. He took it out and stuck it in, took it out and stuck it in, watching the water flow change shape with each move of his hand. His sleeve got soaked.

We put the soap in and then the clothes, and I started to show him how to clean the lint from the dryer trap. He took the fuzzy ball we scraped off and rolled it his hand. "This is so soft," he cooed. Then the soft lint became paste in his wet hand. I told him to go wash his hand. "Then can I watch TV?" he asked.

After that, I kept him away from the laundry room for quite some time. Several years later, when he was going off to be a counselor-in-training at camp, I showed him how to do his own laundry. He did a wonderful job.

At that moment, in the driveway with the recently acquired desk, I realized that my kids should be doing some regular chores, just like kids in the 1950s did. I resolved to start that right away. But not just then, because that whole desk move/dog puke thing had exhausted me. I just wanted to do it myself and get it done.

Day Thirteen—I Think

One afternoon, I was relaxing at the pool, reading a book, when Jack came over to me, fuming and tearful. He had tried to join a stickball game and a kid had told him, "No, you can't play." When he asked why not, the kid said to him, "Because you suck like crap."

At first, I thought this must be some older boy, or a bully. But no, it was a boy Jack's age, eight, who had been a pretty good friend of Jack's last summer. I was caught totally off guard. I didn't know eight-year-olds talked like that. Furthermore, Jack had never played stickball before in his life, so how did that kid know if Jack sucked or not?

Jack was fighting back tears but also piping mad. My first instinct was to march over there to the ball field, give that fresh kid a talking-to, and make sure Jack got to play. But then Jack would get branded as a tattletale and a baby who needs his mama. So then I thought maybe I should find that kid's mom and talk to her about it. But then the kid would get in trouble, and Jack would still be branded a tattletale and a baby.

I put on my cover-up and marched around to a few of my mom friends to tell my story. I could feel my rear end flapping around under my cover-up as I walked, undermining my dignity. Never mind. I was on a mission. My friends were suitably outraged. Their first reaction, like mine, was to interfere and help Jack out. What that kid did was wrong, and a grown-up should fix it.

Or should we? I knew that rough talk and playground battles were part of growing up. I couldn't always make it fair for him. Life is not fair. If this was the 1950s, I would be at home ironing my sheets, not in close enough proximity to solve his problems.

The book I was reading when Jack came over lay open on my chair. I had picked out all kinds of history books, memoirs, and current child-rearing tomes to help guide me through my 1950s summer. I was comparing the two time periods: what was the culture like back then, how did people feel about their lives and their families, and how did parenting today become so suffocating and angst ridden?

Today's book was *A Nation of Wimps* by Hara Estroff Marano. An editor at *Psychology Today* magazine, she had noticed a trend in adolescents: increasing anxiety, depression, immaturity, and delayed independence. She posits that invasive parenting has turned our kids into a bunch of wimps. They can't stand up for themselves or weather setbacks or make decisions. In an effort to make life better for them, we parents have made it too easy for them, and this ultimately makes weak adults.

By now, we all know about snowplow parents. Most of us probably are snowplowers, at least at one time or another. It goes like this: if a kid doesn't study for a test and gets a D, snowplow parents might go talk to the teacher and explain that the kid had a playoff game the night before and was really tired and could he please retake the test? In this way, the parents pave the way for their kids, giving them a smooth ride. It would be better to let the kid suffer through the humiliation of the bad grade and learn that he can bounce back. He will need to work extra hard to pull up his grades after that bad test, and if he does so, he will have the pride of accomplishment and the security in knowing he can rebound from failure.

I had seen many parents snowplow, and it bothered me, but it also made me feel pressured to act in the same manner. After all, if every kid has a parent smoothing the way and pushing them forward, what chance would my kid have to get ahead? Wouldn't I need to smooth and push also?

But I stepped off that merry-go-round, right? I was supposed to be back in the 1950s, when people raised resourceful, resilient kids by letting them handle problems by themselves.

What would I be teaching Jack if I walked over and forced those kids to let him play? I would be teaching him that he is not able to handle his own problems. I would be sending him the message that he is still too young to stand up for himself and that I don't trust him to bounce back from a difficult situation.

What a huge relief this line of thinking provided. *It's not my prob-lem! I don't have to do anything . . . in fact, I am supposed to not do anything! I am simply supposed to think of something tasty for dinner!* The parents of the 1950s had it so easy.

I couldn't just do nothing, though. Poor Jack was miserable. It's one thing to let him handle a problem himself; it's another to ignore your child when they are crying and in distress. I borrowed a Wiffle ball and bat from a mother and got another young boy, and we got our own game going on the grass. Jack got some good hits, and he cheered up, but I knew something was still not right. This was not at all what a 1950s mother would do.

Now I had failed in both decades. I was not practicing confident, hands-off 1950s parenting nor was I successfully butting in to Jack's life with a correct and safe contemporary antibullying message. I was in some weird, ineffectual middle ground in which I didn't stand up for my child, didn't trust him to sort out his own feelings, and was forced to pitch sweaty Wiffle balls to a couple eight-year-olds when I would have preferred to just read my book, which, in perfect irony, was about parenting. Alrighty then.

After twenty minutes, it was too hot to keep playing, and the kids went swimming. I went back to my chair, uneasy that I didn't handle that very well, and worried about Jack. If he never got to play base-ball, would he have a sports inferiority complex? Was he going to be the kid people picked on? Would I ever escape obsessive parenting compulsions?

At dinner that night, Jack told us that later in the day, the "suck like crap" kid tried to get in on a game of tag Jack was starting. Jack told him no because of his earlier "suck like crap" comment. The kid, probably a bit surprised at being so directly confronted, backpedaled and denied that he had been referring to Jack; he tried to make it sound like he had been referring to some other kid. The kid apologized. Then Jack let him play tag.

So Jack handled it on his own after all. He was more resourceful than I thought. I was surprised and then kind of ashamed. Why hadn't I trusted him more? This incident was a clear indication that I could let go and give him more space without worrying. This was exactly the kind of revelation I was hoping for!

Hooray for me. I had decided to go back to the fifties—we were all enjoying it so far. I had decided not to meddle too much in Jack's squabble—and he handled it better than I would have. I felt clear and confident—something I hadn't felt as a parent in a long time.

Euphoric Mom Moments Can Be Fleeting

One morning at the post office, I ran into two moms I knew. Between them, they had five kids, and they were laughing and rolling their eyes at their "relaxing" summer schedule. Camp drop-offs and pickups, baseball travel teams, swim team regionals . . . they barely had time to eat dinner together as a family. They didn't seem unhappy about it, though; they seemed confident and content. Busy equals healthy, right? I had to admit, they looked none the worse for wear. They were dressed in nice shorts, they had fresh pedicures, and they weren't frazzled or cranky. Best of all, their kids were so happy. This one had an award, that one had two new best friends, and another one had read five books since school got out.

I laughed along with the gals, but inside, I crumpled. My pedicure was not fresh. I could never get away from the kids long enough to get to the salon. My children were not winning awards or reading books. Maybe I'd made a horrible mistake; maybe my kids were just going to watch a hideous amount of TV all summer and turn into obese, stupid failures. They'd fall dangerously behind in reading and athletics and never catch up. It would be all my fault.

As I walked home, I gave myself a pep talk. Each family is different, I told myself. This was the right thing for me to do, because my children thrive on yawning days of nothing. They craved TV and hours of free play. They can't abide a schedule. Now I wondered if there was something wrong with my kids.

I was always astounded by the kids, some just eight years old, who would willingly play in two or three hockey games every weekend or happily race through their homework to be finished in time for basketball. Kids who would look forward to a two-hour football practice in full gear in the middle of August. They loved it. There were kids who would beg their parents to sign them up for three-hour art classes and sit attentively during that time. There were kids who read without being told to, who picked up a book and got lost in it because they wanted to. These were not my kids.

As Jack put it: "[Those things] just waste the time I could be relaxing."

Do We Have to Leave, Too?

One of the things I wanted to do this summer was to accept my family for what it was, in all its disorganized, peripatetic "I can burp the alphabet" glory. *My kids are good enough*, I told myself. *Good enough just the way they are.*

Stepping outside the mainstream, I felt alone but also free. I had separated myself from the current mindset, and now I could see how different my kids were from other kids. And if they were that different, then I owed it to them to treat them as such. Maybe that's why all this "keeping up" had felt so hard, because we were just not in that mold. I liked this new feeling of not worrying about what someone else was doing.

Later that afternoon, we went to the pool. We watched four hours of TV in the morning then had lunch and went swimming. The kids were having fun. I was reading a book.

At 4:45 p.m., some moms pulled their kids out of the pool. They had to leave because they had baseball or soccer. Sam looked at me, panicked. "Mom, do we have to leave, too?"

"No, we don't," I said. "You can keep playing."

"Yay!" he shouted and dove underwater.

I adjusted my chair to catch more sun and went back to my book. I was doing what was right for my kids—I hoped.

does childhood
end at eleven?

*What a price! What a picture! . . . Makes you feel like you can
shake hands with the actors!*

—Arvin TV ad, 1955

---

*You spent over six hours today sitting in that stuffy movie
theatre. You could have gone over to the park and played
mumblety-peg!*

—Ward Cleaver,
Leave it to Beaver, "Tenting Tonight," 1958

"SAM!! Your cereal box is blocking the TV!

—Jack, during breakfast

J uly 2nd was Sam's eleventh birthday. It kind of snuck up on me . . . so much for the 1950s making me organized and capable. I took out all of our scheduled activities . . . why did my days still feel so haphazard? All of a sudden, it was July 1st and I was dashing to Target at eight thirty the night before his birthday to buy the toys he wanted then racing home and making a cake from a mix at ten o'clock in the evening. NOT the 1950s.

For his birthday, Sam had asked for action figures, Legos, a Build-A-Bear teddy bear, and a cake covered in strawberry frosting, sprinkles, and chocolate chips. He may have been approaching puberty on the outside, but he was a little boy on the inside.

This was a relief to me, because a few weeks before, I had come across a study done in Britain stating that childhood now ended at age eleven. Yes, that study said most parents believed when a kid reaches the ripe old age of eleven, they're done with toys. They want to listen to music, think about the opposite sex, and sass their parents. In other words, eleven was the new fifteen.

"Pester power" had become so strong that pressured parents would give in to demands by their children to have grown-up privileges, like watching inappropriate movies or dressing provocatively or drinking alcohol. Kids wanted to grow up faster, and parents were too tired to argue.

In the 1950s, parents weren't too tired. They weren't tired because they got married young and had their kids young. I had Sam when I was thirty-five, so the year he turned eleven, I was forty-six. You bet I was tired, and fatigue does affect parenting. For instance, if I would hear my sons cursing in another room, or sneaking a cookie, I'd just pretend not to notice. Not dealing with those things would save my energy so I could deal with something else later, like when the boys were pretending to shoot each other during dinner.

Someday, I thought, Sam and Jack would outgrow shooting each other during dinner. (Let's assume that, at any rate.) In the meantime, they acted like kids, and no amount of encouragement from me had managed to change that.

I hated hearing about this study and felt sorry for kids who got old so fast. I wanted my boys to grow up as slowly as they possibly could without being social misfits. I wanted them to have a childhood so slow and deep it kept them grounded as adults. If it took Sam twenty years to learn how to hold a fork with his fingers instead of his fist or stop gnawing on his dinner roll like a squirrel, so be it.

When Jack told me at age four that "Winnie the Pooh is for babies," my heart sank. A door had closed, and Tigger was out of my life forever. Doors close all the time. That summer, Sam and Jack started to do their own showers, including shampoo. They could get a Band-Aid for themselves. They could call a friend on the phone by themselves and be polite to the grown-up on the other end.

Little by little, they took their steps away from me. Which is as it should be, and I didn't want to be one of those deflated moms mooning around and wondering where her life went when her kids go off to college. I had told myself that I would allow them to grow up slowly, that I would be there for all of it, and that I would feast so richly on those years that I would be able to let go easily when the time came. More likely, I will be half insane from watching Sam eat like a squirrel for twenty years, and hopefully that will make it easier to send him off to college.

In any case, on his eleventh birthday, Sam still loved toys, and he still loved that we hid his presents and gave him clues to find them—a birthday treasure hunt. He skipped around the house batting at draperies and shouting, "I found it!"

He begged me for his favorite blueberry pancakes for breakfast. He ate one and then asked for cereal. Later, we went to meet my mother-in-law at the mall so she could take us all to lunch. He picked TGI Friday's because he had seen it on TV. He refused to order from the kids' menu. "I'm eleven now, Mom," he said. "I'm an adult." Had he read that study from Britain?

He ordered a regular-sized burger off the menu but couldn't finish it. He ordered mozzarella sticks and couldn't finish those, either. He kicked Jack under the table and played with the new action figure he had received that morning. When he and Jack went to the bathroom, Sam crawled under the stall to peer at him and annoy him. They came out of the bathroom shoving and giggling. It was a perfect lunch.

On the way home, we stopped at Build-A-Bear so that Sam could use his gift certificate to select a custom teddy bear. I saw a woman with three boys, each older than Sam. I swear one of them had a mustache. They were all getting bears. Maybe I'm not the only one whose children want to grow up slowly.

I thought about that study. I think that parents who say eleven is the new fifteen simply want their children to grow up faster. They want their kids to eat like adults, to watch TV like adults, to misbehave like adults, because it's easier than having kids. Are they thinking *The faster my kids grow up, the sooner I can get on with my life*? I understand. Children are exhausting and difficult to comprehend, and they slow you down.

But sometimes it's OK to slow down.

That night, my mother called to wish Sam a happy birthday. She asked him how it felt to be eleven. "Kind of exciting," he replied. "Kind of heavy, too."

He knew he was growing up. He just didn't want to rush it.

Plaid, Anyone?

The next day, I had a check-up with my OB/GYN. Jack had a playdate, but Sam had to come with me. I was looking forward to this outing, what with my new "errands are their own kind of fun" attitude. I would get Sam to myself. At that age, when Sam and Jack were in the car together, they would just shout lines from TV shows or beat each other over the head with whatever was in the backseat. But when Sam and I were alone, we would talk. We were just beginning our adult relationship. Last time, he had told me which friends of his used curse words and which curse words they were. This gave him the chance to say the curse words out loud in front of me without getting in trouble. This time, he told me that he wanted to "improve his image as a skateboard guy." He had a skateboard. He never rode it. I didn't bring that up.

While we were in the waiting room, my doctor came out to say hello. Sam stood up and shook the hand of the man who had brought him into this world eleven years and one day ago. The doctor grinned, I grinned, a woman waiting for her appointment grinned. Sam stammered and blinked his eyes. He didn't quite get what all the grinning was about. He didn't understand that to have a healthy baby and watch it grow up is one of life's best miracles. He didn't know that, but the rest of us did, so we stood around grinning and talking about how tall Sam was, wow, he really did get tall. "Yes," I babbled, "his father is tall. I think he just had a growth spurt. Pretty soon, he'll be taller than me." We rambled on about Sam being tall, letting this moment change our day. I was so glad Sam was not in camp right then, that he had come with me to rub his eyes and shuffle his feet while we all appreciated him.

After the doctor appointment, we headed over to the Gap. Sam found a skateboard shirt, which thrilled him. And he agreed to plaid shorts, which made me happy. With his tan and his bleached-blond hair and his plaid Bermudas, he looked like a preppy little beach bum. I liked the way his ramshackle personality was unfolding, but I was not above wanting to coax him into certain behaviors or lifestyles. In the plaid shorts, for example, he looked like he would be a sailing instructor at summer camp and then go on to attend Duke University as a successful engineering student and campus heartthrob. This would all be followed by a lucrative career and a well-groomed family. You can get a lot from plaid shorts. I bought a pair for Jack, too. Plaid shorts have been around since the 1950s. They have staying power.

Let's Play Life

One of the things I wanted to do this summer with my kids was to play more board games. What could be more 1950s than sitting around on the living room floor enjoying Yahtzee? It's the picture of wholesome family togetherness. Indeed, our family has had some of our best times playing board games together, even if Jack did cry when he lost. In fact, he would start crying when it looked like he might possibly lose, even if it was only his third turn. He needed to work on sportsmanship.

In the years since our 1950s summer, board games have faded from our family life. It went from "Hooray, we're going to play a family game!" to "Well, OK, but which family game?" to "Do we have to? I'm tired, and I have homework!" Our family activities shifted to center around watching movies together—which was fun, but not at all the same as sprawling on the floor with our dog walking through the board and upsetting the pieces and getting to argue over whose turn it was. When the boys became teens, the only time we played board games was when there was a power outage and nothing else to do. We usually had fun, and Sam would say, "We should do this more often!" But we didn't.

It takes time and energy to play board games, and during this slow summer, we had plenty of time, so one afternoon, we played the board game Life.

I can remember summer afternoons from my childhood, my sister and I sitting on our friend Betty's screened porch, playing hours and hours of Life. Bill and I bought the game for the kids the previous Christmas, because it is such a classic. But in the six months since then, we'd never had the time to play it. Every time the kids had asked to play it, we had to say "Pick another game; Life is too long." But now, with a whole afternoon to fill, Life was perfect.

I had to read the instructions all over again because I had forgotten how to play it. Right off the bat, you have to choose whether you are going to go to college or begin a career. Along the way, the spin of the wheel decides whether you will get married or have children and various other ups and downs. As we played, I watched my children make "life" choices with a mixture of dread and delight.

Jack chose to start a career right away; he didn't want any delay in getting a salary. He was good with money, and to this day, he always has plenty in his piggy bank. He was always the most frequent winner in the family game of Toy Story Monopoly, as he amassed dollars and smacked his hands together like a little mogul.

Sam chose college, which relieved me. He was old enough to realize that is the responsible choice. But poor Sam is terrible with money. Even though he went to college and Jack entered the workforce right away, the career cards they drew gave Jack a lucrative computer job and Sam became a teacher with limited resources. I watched them drive along in their little plastic cars, deciding what houses to buy, collecting money, and paying taxes. Jack got married. Sam did, too. Then Jack had a couple of kids. But Sam kept missing those spaces. As the game wore on, it became clear that Sam was never going to have children. He was very upset by this. "When am I going to have children?" he would wail. "I want to have kids! Jack has a bigger house than me and two kids! It's not fair!"

At first, I thought it was funny that he was taking the game so seriously. But then I got caught up in it and started imagining their real lives, their real futures. I suddenly saw the years of suffering and disappointment that are possible for us all. Sam loves children. What if he really never did have a family? It would break his heart. What if I don't like his wife? I know plenty of people who don't get along with their son- or daughter-in-law. Their future unfolded before me: Sam and Jack moving out, starting careers, having problems. They would move to other cities and hardly ever see each other. They could be stumbling or kind of lost, and I wouldn't know about it. How would I help them then?

I saw Sam, my sweet, exuberant Sam, pouring his energy and creativity into a job that doesn't pay very much, being unappreciated, coming home to a sparsely furnished apartment, and just staring at his flat-screen TV. The walls are a drab white; he hasn't even bothered to paint or decorate. He rustles up something to eat or calls a friend. His wife is away on business, and he misses her, but at least tonight they won't have a tense discussion about fertility treatments. Maybe he'll play some video games and stay up too late. Or maybe he'll realize he needs to do laundry and head out to the laundromat at around eight o'clock. He will strike up a conversation with whomever is there and make them laugh, because that's how he is. He has to make people laugh. Then he'll go home. I hope he has some plans for the weekend.

I see Jack in a comfortable home in the suburbs. He has a nice family . . . but he works so hard. Twelve hours a day. He likes it, and he makes good money, but the stress is getting to him. He is becoming a little withdrawn because of all this stress, and his wife is worried about him. They never just relax and have fun anymore. Lately Jack has been wondering: Is this all there is? Shouldn't I be enjoying myself more? He calls up Sam, his brother who can always make him laugh. Sam is at the laundromat, but he picks up his cell, and they have a few good chuckles. They've got to get together soon, they agree. Maybe over Thanksgiving, if the airfares aren't too expensive. They hang up. Jack goes down to the basement to check the furnace and wonders why he feels so blue.

Why did we play this stupid game? We should have just played Yahtzee! My children, my beautiful, happy boys, are going to grow up and be subjected to all manner of sadness and pain. Drudgery, anxiety, loneliness, and regret—not to mention a variety of possible traffic or boating accidents—and I can't protect them. I can't stop them from making mistakes, from being at risk, from wondering what on earth they have done with their lives.

Thank God we have this summer, I consoled myself. This precious summer, when we can just cocoon with each other and enjoy the days as they are. No matter what, we'll always have these days, these memories, this deliberate, layered childhood that will serve as a touchstone for them as they age, a place of safety and strength they can return to in their minds, and I will take comfort in the fact that despite the distance or trouble that the years may bring, once upon a time, I gave my sons a gift of time and togetherness.

The fact is, years later, the kids barely remembered this summer. The lazy days blended into a collective summer memory that included all nice summer memories. For me, it stood as a clear choice I made and relished—it changed my worldview. For them, they loved living it but easily let it go.

The game ended. Jack won, a satisfied little millionaire. Sam came in last—that is, he had the least money. I came in second. In my panicky, emotional state, I tried to think of something else we could all play together to stave off the despair of their future lives, to take advantage of these safe, golden moments. But the boys were already wrestling and fighting over who had to put away the game. "Winner cleans up!" "No, loser does!"

My reverie snapped, and I began yelling at them to both clean up, then to take that energy outside in the backyard for a while. They scrambled around, falling over each other, shoving the bits back into the box in a haphazard manner. They had to use the bathroom. They needed a drink. They ran upstairs for a magic wand. They got a cape and a Darth Vader mask. They ran outside. The dog followed them. We brought the dog back in before he could pee on the lawn. The house got quiet. I realized that I was happy to have them outside.

Playing Life reminded me how little we control. Parenting today is a cavalcade of micromanagement as we peer over our kids' shoulders and monitor their playtime, their schoolwork, their reading choices, their text messages, their friends, their outdoor safety, and their sports endeavors. They do nothing outside our purview. And yet, what guarantee does all that control bring? At some point, they will be on their own. No matter how many sports you made them play, they might become fat and sedentary. No matter how much you kept them away from TV or video games, they may become a Grand Theft Auto addict. No matter how you instilled good grooming and style, they might spend their adulthood in flip-flops and stubble. No matter how often you drill them about safe driving, they might jump in the car without buckling up and text while driving to the grocery store. We really don't control that much.

When I thought about that, it filled me with relief rather than panic.

Giving up control sounded great to me. All that control is exhausting, and if it doesn't work anyway, what's the point?

I love my children so much more intensely than I ever imagined I could love, and I don't want them hurt. I don't care about a bad test grade or a broken arm. I am worried about an unhappy marriage, a spinal cord injury, a failed career. To love this deeply is daily torture. You are so vulnerable. To let yourself love like that is to suffer constantly.

After careening through their futures for the past few hours, I tried to find myself again. I read the mail. I folded some laundry. I checked the weather channel. Gradually, I returned to the here and now. I started dinner so I could think about chicken cutlets instead of the terror of loving deeply.

I'm a Frump!

Thinking about the 1950s made me want to indulge in housewife fantasy. What if my home could be adorable, welcoming, and well run? What would it feel like to be organized, ready for each day, with enough free time to style my hair and select a shirt and pants that look good together? I usually threw on anything that was clean and didn't even look in the mirror before racing off to the grocery store.

What my 1950s counterpart would wear on an ordinary day:

- Dress (ironed)
- Apron (ironed)
- Hose with a girdle/garters
- Leather flats
- Necklace/earrings
- Hat
- Gloves
- Full face of makeup

Wow. Couldn't I do better than day-old yoga pants and a T-shirt? Being sloppily dressed was just one of the many ways my standard of living had become subpar. Since I was always racing to the next moment, nothing about the present moment ever mattered. Who cared if my T-shirt was stained or my hair needed washing? The main thing was to get out the door and get everyone where they needed to be! This same philosophy carried over to my house. I didn't change the sheets regularly, just whenever I thought about it. At any given time, there were pajamas on my living room floor because the boys were so dawdling and contrary that I had developed the habit of carrying their clothes for the day down to the living room and letting them get dressed in front of the TV. Then they would go into the powder room on the first floor to brush their teeth. I actually kept an extra set of toothbrushes and toothpaste in the powder room so that they could brush their teeth there every morning. If I made them go upstairs, they would simply get distracted by whatever toys were lying about and end up playing on the floor until I charged up the stairs, shouting, "WHAT IS TAKING SO LONG?" So I simply hovered around them like a backstage dresser to an opera star, handing them clothes and toothbrushes and a comb, just so that we could get out the door on time.

I had forsaken order because of our schedule . . . we had to go to soccer practice or karate class or a piano lesson. Those things were much more important than any type of daily living standard.

But in the 1950s, pleasant daily living was a practiced art form, especially for housewives, and I longed to tackle some neglected household tasks. I wanted to give the dining room a makeover, clean out a few closets, and organize all our photos into albums. I had hoped these weeks of summer would be the perfect time for all that.

Yeah, right. Summer is the WORST time for projects. First of all, the kids are out of school and hanging around all day, constantly asking for food. Second, we spent four hours a day at the pool. Third, there is the natural inertia of summer. It is hot. It is humid. Your body is telling you to take it easy, not climb a ladder and spackle.

With my new relaxed attitude, though, household harmony seemed possible. Less meddling in the kids' lives should have meant more time to fuss over my own. I wanted to turn over a new leaf and give my children the opportunity to grow up in a well-kept home. They should have some standards so that they become accustomed to cleanliness and order. At that point, they were accustomed to chaos and dust.

One day, I was tidying up, and I made the kids turn off the TV and help me. "We need to clean up," I told them. "Why?" asked Jack. "Is someone coming over?"

You see, they saw cleaning as something you did when company was coming over, not a regular part of decent living. So, yes, I wanted to do a better job of running the house. And I wanted to do some fun projects, hopefully ones that I could involve the boys in—like the photo albums.

I had two years of photographs in shopping bags. These photographs were left over from the years before we got a digital camera, when I used to print out every roll of film, in doubles, and then put them in a drawer until I found the time to put them into an album. Then the drawer would fill up, so I'd move them to a cabinet, then two cabinets, then they started spilling out on the floor when I opened the cabinet door. Finally, in a rush, and completely irate at the endless amount of crap that was everywhere, I shoved them all into two giant shopping bags and stuck them in a corner in my bedroom.

Before I knew it, I was four years behind in putting photos in albums. I imagined that Sam and Jack would *love* looking at all these old pictures with me. I envisioned us gathered snugly around the dining room table, happily reliving our precious family moments. We'd glow with warmth as we saw ourselves at our past Halloween parties, dressed up as Ninjas and eating fried chicken. We'd giggle with nostalgia as we revisited many Christmas Eves, enjoying big Uncle Eddie in his Santa suit joking and handing out gifts.

I bounded into the living room. "Hey, you guys, want to put some pictures in photo albums? We can look at our trip to Hershey and remember all our Halloween parties! We'll see Uncle Eddie in the Santa suit! It'll be fun!"

They didn't even look up. "Um, do we have to?" "Can't we just play?"

Oh, well, I thought. *I'll try again in a few weeks. We have all summer.*

The Perfect Family

I know we're not supposed to compare ourselves to other people, but we all do it. It's our way of checking up on ourselves, making sure we are on the right track. Part of my goal that summer was to be different from everyone else, to step off the conformity track and pave my own way. But when the Fourth of July came around, I found myself with expectations. I wanted to be a *perfect family.*

The perfect family is what you see in all the Fourth of July advertisements. Perfect Family loves parades. Perfect Family loves to decorate their bikes with red, white, and blue streamers. Perfect Dad is not emotionally invested in his lawn, so he loves to spend all day with the kids, taking in a ball game, or doing cannonballs at the pool. Perfect Mom is well rested and organized; she has already done all the grocery shopping and has plenty of delicious chips, steaks, and popsicles. She has clean, adorable red, white, and blue clothes for everyone in Perfect Family to wear that day. Perfect Children love the crowds at carnivals, don't mind standing in line for the Moon Bounce, and are so excited by the festive outdoor activities of the nation's birthday that they have no interest at all in TV. Perfect Family loves a good fireworks show. They have a couple of big blankets and know just where to put them to get the best view. Perfect Children are respectfully awed, not frightened, by the loud bangs and flashes. They love to sit still on the blanket, not whine or run around bored out of their minds at the noisy, stupid fireworks.

We got up early on the Fourth because Sam and Bill, as Boy Scout and Leader, were marching in the town parade. They looked spiffy in their uniforms. Perfect. Jack and I grabbed a couple of chairs and walked down to the end of our block because our house is close to the route. We saw a lot of our friends. Perfect.

Perfect ended there. Jack and I were wearing green or orange or whatever was on top in the drawer. It was humid, and Jack was whining. The marchers threw candy, and Jack could never catch it. I had Oliver, and he barked his head off in a totally obnoxious manner at all the police sirens, fire truck sirens, ambulance sirens, and high school marching band horn sections. Jack covered his ears and rolled up in a ball. People stared. We went home.

Bill and Sam came home in their uniforms, hot and cranky. They just wanted to peel off their clothes and flake out in front of the air conditioner. The day went like this: Bill surfed the Internet for two hours and disappeared into the backyard to edge and fertilize until dusk. Sam fiddled around in his room and then got dressed up in a suit, tie, and sunglasses to play secret agent by himself in the backyard. Jack whined to watch his fifth hour of TV, and when I said no, he cried until he fell asleep on the sofa and took a two-hour nap. I pulled apart bedrooms and vacuumed behind dressers. When dinner came, nobody wanted to eat the steaks I bought. Nobody wanted to go to the fireworks. We ate pizza and played the Wii.

When you're sitting around the pool talking about what you did on the Fourth of July, there are various status rankings for your activities:

High status: You were at the shore. That means you got out of town and can imply that someone in your family owns a beach house to which you have regular access. You watched the fireworks from a blanket on the sand, embers falling dramatically into the pounding surf.

Acceptable status: You hosted/attended a fun barbecue. This shows that you and your family are well adjusted socially and have plenty of well-adjusted, social friends. It shows you planned ahead and enjoy doing things as a family. You watched the fireworks at the local park, surrounded by other families, secure in the love of good friends and our country.

Low status: You just had a quiet time with family at the pool or a ball game and then ate hamburgers in the backyard. This would show that you, while perhaps not super social, are at least patriotic enough to observe the holiday in the traditional family-oriented, grilled-meat fashion. You watched the fireworks from the front lawn with a few trees blocking the view.

Failure: You stayed home and each pursued your own cleaning, napping, mowing, and secret agent agenda, without speaking to each other for hours, and then huddled around the air conditioner with your pizza. At least one of you never even showered that day, but I'm not saying who. You didn't watch the fireworks—not even on TV—because the kids preferred to play a video game. You heard the fireworks in the distance, though, and the dog went nuts barking at them until the noise got so bad you just wished the stupid Fourth was over already.

Everybody likes quirky; nobody likes weird. If in fact, it had been the 1950s, we could have been called into the McCarthy hearings for celebrating the Fourth in this manner.

The 1950s have a reputation of suffocating conformity, but believe me, there is plenty of conformity in this day and age, too. By removing the super-structure of schedule and programmed activities and allowing our summer to unfold in its own organic way, I was able to see my family clearly for what we are. We are a family of complete nonconformists. Not the cool nonconformists—we're not The Fonz. We're the uncool nonconformists. We are a family that on Super Bowl Sunday wonders if there is a good movie on. We are a family who while at Disney World skips half the rides just to go back to the hotel and swim for three hours. We are a family who keeps a plastic penguin in the freezer because, well, penguins like it cold.

I know that I'm different. I've always felt like an outsider: too bour-geois to be an artsy person and too offbeat to be comfortable in the regular crowd. It's taken me a long time to be comfortable with the fact that no crowd is really my home. I've made my peace with it. But it bothers me to think of my children as different, as never fitting in, because it seems so much easier to belong. Of course, they will grow up and be who they're meant to be, and being comfortable in your own skin is the most important thing. But I was hoping it would be easier for them.

I didn't tell anyone that my family doesn't like fireworks and that my husband would rather aerate the soil than go to a neighbor's cook-out. I didn't see any reason to invite scrutiny. So when people asked me, later in the week, how my Fourth was, I just said, "It was great. How was yours?" And I left it at that.

whose vacation is it, anyway?

Joan and Bob just returned from a honeymoon . . . only four-teen days . . . but it was plenty of time to visit England, France, Switzerland, Italy and Portugal. Flying made it possible!

—Douglas Airplanes ad, 1952

You're in a rut. Life is oozing by, and suddenly you'll be an old woman and you'll say to yourself, "What happened?"

—Myrtle, a neighbor,
Father Knows Best, "Margaret Goes Dancing," 1954

Mom, you need some relaxing lessons. I could teach you.

—Jack

Our beach week had arrived. It was the time each year when we headed to North Carolina for a week with my parents, my siblings, and all of our children. We looked forward to it all year long: the kids would see their cousins and I would see my sister and brother for what is usually the only time during the whole year. We would stay in a big house on a quiet island. It was always fun and exciting—the centerpiece of our summer. We couldn't wait. But first, we had to get ready.

I had been looking especially forward to the trip this year because of my 1950s experiment. The setting down in North Carolina was like something out of the past. There are geckos, snakes, pelicans, crabs, giant water bugs, and cabbage head jellyfish everywhere. It's the perfect place for young boys who aren't afraid to touch stuff. Plus, that year there was a brand new bike path that ran the length of the island. Jack was still learning to ride, but I knew he'd get it any time. *We will love riding that bike path*, I thought. I felt my 1950s summer was going well and that I was ready to take it to a whole new level. But first, we had to get ready.

A Mom Is Prepared

If you've ever readied a husband, two kids, and a dog for a week at the beach, you know there's a bit of planning involved. It starts the week before. That's when you have to get the car checked out and somehow manage to pay for the unexpected new tires you need the very same week you are going to pay for a beach rental. You have to make sure all the prescriptions are refilled and up to date, including the ones for the dog, so he doesn't throw up on the way to the perfect vacation. You have to check out movies and books on tape from the library to entertain yourselves on the eleven-hour drive to the beach. And you have to do laundry. You have to wash every single thing you might even consider bringing.

You do all this because you have to be prepared. *You are the mom.* So you need to make sure that in case your young child runs a fever, you have the digital ear thermometer, the children's Advil with measuring spoon, and a printout of all the local doctors that are on your insurance plan.

Never mind that you can never be totally prepared. When your eight-year-old turns to you and says, "Mom, did we bring Wiseguy?" you will have to say no, we didn't. Wiseguy is a little stuffed penguin that somehow did not make the short list of fifty stuffed animals that came with us. Wiseguy is at home in humid New Jersey, wedged under the bed, instead of here, at a sunny beach house in North Carolina, wedged under the bed.

When it rains, you have windbreakers. When it is chilly on the deck at night, you have sweatshirts. When they pee themselves laughing during a sleepover with their cousins at midnight, you have extra pajamas. You even have enough extra everything for their cousins, too.

You also have ten magazines and four books you have been dying to read. You have these things because, even after all these years, you still allow yourself to think that you are going to read on your vacation. You allow the fantasy of "a week at the beach" to seduce you into thinking that you are going to relax. And then, halfway through the week, when you haven't cracked even one book and you pass out cold, exhausted, every night at ten o'clock, you will think, *Oh yeah, I forgot. Moms don't relax on vacation.*

The image of moms who do everything for their families and are totally fulfilled by it seems rooted in the 1950s image of family, but it is a reality in these times, too. We give lip service to the idea that we moms need to "take some time for ourselves," but that doesn't happen often, especially when your children are young and especially when you're on vacation. Little kids can't put on their own suntan lotion, and they can't hang up their bathing suits or wet towels because they can't reach the clotheslines. They certainly don't pack for themselves. If they did, mine would travel with a bunch of Legos, a blankie, and a single pair of SpongeBob boxers.

The need to be prepared has been intensified by my generation of mothers into the need to *control*. We have ramped up the mothering. No longer content enough to adopt a defensive stance of being pre-pared with things just in case, we now adopt an offensive position, a series of aggressive game plans designed to forestall anything bad that might come our way. For instance, when I was a little girl and we drove to the beach in the late 1960s, there were three of us kids and a large poodle in the backseat. I don't remember wearing seatbelts—being in the backseat was safe enough. We bounced all over the car, we waved out the back window to other drivers, and when we got too noisy, one of my parents would threaten to reach back and give us a swat.

Back in the 1950s, taking a big car trip was a new and exciting way to vacation. Americans drove several hundred billion miles each year during that decade. They paid about twenty-four cents for a gallon of gas, and they enjoyed eating at the brand-new roadside restaurants like McDonald's and Kentucky Fried Chicken. They played the license plate game or had a sing-along with the family to pass the time.

Fifty years later, as we headed to the beach, we would belt the kids in tightly, strap a DVD player to the seat, plant some headphones over their ears, and anesthetize them with movies for the entire ride. The only time we even spoke to them was to let them know that we were going to pull over and they need to put their shoes back on so they could get out and go to the bathroom. They had snacks, pillows, and plenty of water with a secure lid on top all within their easy reach so they would not distract me from navigating the most direct route or helping my husband to conduct the safest driving possible. If, for a few seconds, the kids touched each other, or fought over controlling the remote, or argued about which movie to watch next, Bill would get so instantly stressed that little veins would appear at his temples and he would snarl, "That has to stop NOW!" His safe driving was threatened.

It's not that things are more dangerous these days; it's that there are more ways to control things now. Seatbelts, airbags, GPS, Purell, Airborne spray, fortified juice, organic cleaning products—all designed to swoon us into the idea that nothing bad ever has to happen.

A Mom Has Everything Under Control—or Does She?

It is easy enough to control things when you are at home. You have a routine, and on any given day, you have a pretty good idea of what places, people, and situations your children will encounter. You have already taken the measures necessary to adjust these situations to your level of comfort, and your days can pass without too many surprises.

When you go on vacation to the beach with your extended family, things are much different. Every family has different rules about drinking soda, eating vegetables, bicycle helmets, swimming, and boating safety. Your ability to dictate to your child will be limited now that he sees how other families function. "But Sarah doesn't have to eat carrots!" Just give up. It's vacation.

The one thing that has always bothered me is the ocean. Where we stay, the beach is private and there are no lifeguards. There is also a prominent sign at the entrance to the beach that warns DANGEROUS CURRENTS AND RIPTIDES—SWIM AT YOUR OWN RISK. I don't want my children to swim at their own risk. I want them to swim in safe, placid little waves with lifeguards, rafts, flotation devices, and an oxygen tent standing by.

They want to swim in loud, rough surf. Getting pushed by the waves and ending up with a snoot full of salty water is fun. Bobbing up and down past the breakers is exhilarating. Every year, they want to go out farther, ride the waves more boldly, and stay in longer.

My anxiety would start in early spring. Terrifying visions of drowning children began popping into my head. I would see myself standing on the beach, helpless, while Sam or Jack was being pulled out to sea, his head disappearing for the last time. I scream, but no one can hear me over the surf. I try to swim out to get him, but the roiling ocean is so dark, I can't find him. Then I would see myself on the sand as the helicopters land and the rest of us huddle on the beach while the rescue search begins. I would be sick from fear and desperation.

It's kind of hard to enjoy a day at the beach when you come from this vantage point.

I had expressed my anxiety to the rest of the family, and they were sympathetic, but no one wanted to change the venue. Like all of us, my sister has anxieties of her own, so she is sympathetic, but her kids swim in these waters all the time, and she is used to it. She would help arrange things so that we didn't go to the beach every day and only on days when the riptide risk was low. Other days, we would go the pool, or bike, or go fishing, and some days, it would rain and we'd be inside anyway. It worked out very well because the kids were so happy just being with their cousins, anything we did was fine with them. But my whole trip was always overshadowed by the anxiety of ocean swimming.

Anxiety affects us all to some degree. Every parent I know has overblown fears about something, or in many cases, lots of things, all stoked by the twenty-four-hour news cycle. Fear of abduction and pedophiles is a popular one and is fanned to a frenzy by the media. Fear of traffic accidents and fear of disease ("Is *E. coli* on Your Kitchen Counter?") are other biggies. And then there are lesser fears—the ones parents have always had—fear of your child doing badly in school ("State Math Scores Lower Than Ever!") or getting into trouble ("Dangerous Apps Your Child Might Download!").

With those kinds of messages blabbing in our ears, it is no wonder we've all become a bunch of hothouse parents.

I had to decide which days were the safest to go to the ocean, and on the days that we went, I hovered next to Sam and Jack as they played in the surf, shouting over the waves at them—come back this way, you're out too far, you're drifting with the current. No matter how tired I was, I would fight the waves with them, to be near them—just in case. Moms don't relax on vacation.

A Mom Makes Sure Everyone Has Fun

The best part of a beach house vacation is having your whole family—three generations—together under one roof. The hardest part of a beach house vacation is having your whole family—three generations—together under one roof. Everybody has different expectations for their vacation, and they don't always match up.

My parents would always look forward to this week as a time of early morning beach walks, quiet conversations on the deck, afternoons reading good books or dozing, and a few nice dinners in good restaurants. My children would look forward to this week as a time of the loudest hide-and-seek games possible, having swordfights outside with their shirts off, and laughing so hard during lunch that potato chips shoot out of their mouths in a fine spray.

My parents wanted to spend some time on the beach with their grandchildren. They wanted to watch them swim strongly in the surf, or skim-board with skill, or reel in a fish that Uncle Paul helped them catch. What they saw instead was Sam skim-boarding out of control until he crashed into my ankle and I cursed at him. They saw the cousins throw wet sand at each other until Jack got it in his eye. They witnessed the kids disobediently pretend they couldn't hear me when I frantically shouted that they were out too far in the waves.

On a typical day, my parents would be looking forward to some nice family time on the deck around five thirty and then a good dinner with interesting conversation. In actuality, at five thirty, everyone was just straggling in from various activities and trying to get cleaned up. My sister and I would get the kids through their post-swim toilette pretty rapidly. Then they would flake out in front of the TV, slack jawed and with low blood sugar, until we called them for dinner. Bill would lock himself in the bathroom to complete his post-swim toilette, which typically took forty-five minutes. My post-swim toilette, like all my toilettes, takes six and one-half minutes.

We would gather without Bill, and then he would come out and start to cook dinner, which, as I believe I have already mentioned, takes him three hours. He loves to cook, so he drags it out for his own enjoyment. On nights like that, we fed the kids early.

The kids sucked down some chicken nuggets and watermelon off of paper plates, got an immediate second wind, and started racing through the house, deck, and driveway screaming at the top of their lungs. My sister and I got out some crackers and cheese to get enough energy to round up the kids. We put the kids in pajamas and made them watch a movie, then we ate our steak at nine thirty and staggered into bed soon after. Bill and my dad, however, would relax on the deck late into the evening, discussing the various battles of World War II and looking at the stars.

Amidst the commotion, we all found the enduring connections that we craved. My father and Bill shared some much-needed "guy time," the kids had wild play with their cousins, and I got the sublime mother/sister closeness that I missed all year long.

A Mom Makes Sure Memories Are Made

My children loved the big house and the pool and the ocean and all the activities, but what they really loved was their cousins. They loved having their grandparents around, but they hardly talked to them because they were busy playing with their cousins. The feeling of three generations under one roof, in a place they came back to year after year, gave them a sense of belonging and continuity.

The beach vacation started out as something fun to do, but it ended up being a cornerstone for all of us, proving to me that investing time and energy into my family will always pay dividends I can hardly imagine at the time. As time went on and the kids became teenagers, we had to work the beach week around sleepaway camps and summer jobs. One summer, we canceled the week altogether. It seemed like the only recourse at the time—there was simply no compatible time period when we were all available. It left a hole in our year, a feeling of loss; something had been skipped. During one particularly stressful day of November that year, my husband said, "Why didn't we go to the beach this summer? I needed that!" The rest of his year just didn't feel right.

On one of our early beach trips, when Sam was about four, we were all on the beach in the late afternoon. These were the days that the kids were too young to go out into the surf and instead just played at the water's edge. Late afternoon was the most beautiful time to be down there. My mother, little Sam, and I took a long stroll down the beach, collecting the occasional shell and singing little songs. My mother and Sam held hands and marched and sang a little made-up song. Later that evening, we were sitting on the deck before dinner, and Sam was still humming the little song. My mother looked up, smiled, and said to Sam, "Will you remember that walk for the rest of your life? I will."

At the time, my mother was about seventy. Of course she could remember that walk for the rest of her life. Sam, at four, would most likely not remember it. The thing they created together, a little walk in the sand, was now a precarious little memory, able to last and be nurtured or capable of being swept away. Of course my mother knew that Sam would not be able to remember that walk for the rest of his life; she was just teasing him. But she was absolutely serious about the fact that she would remember, and that made the memory stick.

This is the real reason for family vacations: not to relax, but to make memories. Our children think that beach house is the most special place in the world. They have grown up there. They began in diapers there and used to sit naked at the water's edge and eat sand. Both Sam and Jack learned to put their face under water there and got comfortable with jumping into the deep end of the pool. In 2004, we celebrated my parents' 50th wedding anniversary there with a small family party. Sam, then age seven, wore a jacket and tie and danced with me. By the time of my 1950s summer, he and his cousin Sarah both had iPods, and they would listen to music and talk instead of running around playing superheroes. Sarah had braces on her teeth. Many summers had passed.

That year was the beginning of an end of an era. My father had been diagnosed with Alzheimer's. The beach house was the first time we had all been together since his diagnosis, and it was a chance to come together and talk about it. In the living room, my dad held a conference. My mother took the grandkids to the pool so the adults could speak freely about it all. My dad's main concern was that my mother would have all the support she needed. We asked questions and offered assurances, and then there was not much else to say. We all knew what lay ahead. We ended up going to the pool. It was a beautiful day, and those don't last forever.

My parents were married in 1954 and had my brother in 1957. They are truly parents from the 1950s, and they fit the classic profile. My dad was among the first in his family to graduate college; he served time in the Marine Corps and, after getting his MBA, began work at a big accounting firm. He and my mother had met in college and married right afterward, moving to Camp Pendleton so my father could serve his enlistment in the Marines. I had been thinking of the 1950s as frozen in time, a place I wanted to visit, but to my parents, the '50s were a passage. It was their jumping-off point, the place from which they accelerated into their future. They had plans. They had a family; they bought houses; they pursued careers; they traveled; they put us all through college and helped us move away; they attended our weddings. And then they got the idea to have a big family beach vacation every year.

Each year, we came and made memories. Nothing that spectacular. More like, remember when Jack caught that fish and it pooped on him? Remember when Sam fell on his Heelys and missed Bingo Night because he needed stitches? Remember when Jack and Jacob rode bikes in their pajamas? Remember when Pauley, just learning to walk, would go back and forth through the screen door for hours, letting it slam behind him?

For my children, these memories became a foundation, a way of knowing who they were and where they came from. For my parents, these memories were a fulfillment, a result of the love and energy they have devoted to their family. For me, these memories were a gift that I gave to myself and others. I worked hard to make those beach weeks fun, but sometimes I could not appreciate the memories I was creating at the time; I was too tired. I figured I would enjoy them one day and be grateful for the hours spent creating them. I was right.

As my father's illness progressed, my parents left their home in Maryland and moved down to North Carolina. They bought a house near my sister. During our beach vacation week, my mom would bring Dad to the house for lunch and the afternoon. His eyes would light up in recollection at the sight of the huge clock in the kitchen, the giant marlin mounted on the wall, the map over the fireplace. He recognized the serene view from the deck, and we could discuss how the flag was waving in the distance or hear the wind in the palm trees. Since Alzheimer's patients don't remember things, you can't talk about stuff that you did last year or even earlier in the day. But talking about something that is happening at the moment, right in front of you, is extremely rewarding. So we could talk about the paddle boarder rowing by or the beautiful cloud formations. These were things we had always talked about on the deck.

He passed away in February of 2014. We had a private cremation ceremony, and afterward, the immediate family went to the beach house to have lunch. We sat around the table eating chicken salad that a friend had dropped off. It was too cold to be out on the deck, but we looked out the window at the flag, and the water, and the trees. The living room seemed empty and full at the same time.

We had spent only one or two weeks a year in that house, but its memories are as deep and permanent as anything in this world can be. Perhaps because they were summer memories, and summer has its own magic. Perhaps because those weeks were a time of slowness and family and truly paying attention.

A Mom Rejoices When All the Pieces Come Together to Create Perfection

The bike path is beautiful. It is smooth blacktop, weaving through sand and beach grass alongside the road by houses or little inlets. It is a delight to ride. I couldn't wait to ride it all together—just as soon as Jack learned how.

Teaching Jack to ride a bike had not been easy. Jack hates to learn anything new; that is, he hates trying or struggling. He wants to do something right the first time or give up and watch TV.

Plus, he was scared. Scared of falling, scared of getting hurt, scared of that weird, flying feeling you get when you start to get going on your bike.

I knew, though, when he finally got it, he would love it. What kid doesn't? So I'd been pushing him along to learn. I had tried the year before, but it didn't work. This spring, we had been insisting he keep trying, using this new bike path as incentive. I had a vision of us all, tanned and fit, riding single file along the path in our crisp, ironed shirts. Our teeth were so white! We were so happy! We were a beautiful, bike-riding, everybody-loves-each-other 1950s family.

About a week before we left for vacation, I took Jack down to the swim club parking lot before the pool opened so we could practice riding. At ten in the morning, it was already blazing hot, and his helmet was making his head itch, and his sandals kept slipping off the pedals, and he wailed dramatically whenever his shin got slapped by a pedal. "I CAN'T DO IT!" he bellowed. "I'LL NEVER BE ABLE TO DO THIS!"

Sweat was pooling in my bra, and I was annoyed and embarrassed at his total lack of persistence. For heaven's sake, how will this kid ever finish college or hold down a job? He gives up so easily!

I alternated between saying things like "Stop whining; everybody has trouble when they learn" and "Good, good! See, you almost had it!" Neither of us was having much fun. Then I saw a man walking his dog on the other side of the parking lot. He was watching us wistfully.

Perhaps he was remembering those halcyon days when he first learned to ride or when he taught his own kids. He was on the outside looking in, and what he saw was magic. He saw the miracle that is riding a bike, the miracle of learning something risky and wonderful, the miracle of helping someone grow up. Suddenly, through his eyes, I saw it, too. I saw what I was really doing. I was loving my son.

At the beach house, there is a long, smooth driveway which feeds right onto a deserted cul-de-sac. It is the perfect place to learn to ride, and now Jack was good enough to try on his own. I didn't have to constantly hold on. I felt victorious because this was *just how I planned it*. I did something right. I was an excellent mother. And sure enough, it clicked. After a few days of trying, Jack was riding. He could even get started himself without a steadying hand. He straddled the bike with his feet on the ground, inched forward until the right pedal was just the correct height and the left pedal was just so, until he felt confident pushing off.

Our family could all go for a ride on the bike path! I fulfilled the picture in my head! Sam rode ahead, showing off, and Bill kept up with him. I hung back with Jack, who stopped often and had to restart. "Jack," I said. "We don't have to do the whole path. It's pretty hot out now."

"I don't care if the sweat is pouring down my face," he said. "I'm doing the whole path." Did I detect determination?

He got going, a little wobbly, then faster, and then he even took a little hill at some speed without flinching. My heart felt light and fluttery as I watched him pedal ahead of me. He was having fun. He was not scared anymore. He was on his own, air all around him, accelerating into his own future.

fine, dear; now go outside and play

From the first you light . . . to your last at night . . . Old Golds treat your taste right . . . all day long!

—Old Gold Cigarettes ad, 1952

You'd better light up, Tom. It's going to be a long evening.

—Jim Anderson to his guest, Tom,
Father Knows Best, "Matchmaker," 1955

Mom! Is it true that Pop Pop smoked?

—Sam

Our vacation was over, and we returned from North Carolina. It was always a letdown—knowing our yearly vacation is over and we have to wait twelve more months to have another one stinks. The mechanics of getting back to regular life were a drag, too. The drive home seemed a lot longer than the drive going down there. The house was hot and musty when we got back; there was no food; mountains of laundry waited to be done. The laundry smelled like the beach and made me miss vacation even more. We unloaded the car and stacked all the bags in the front hall. I ran out to the store to get milk for the morning, and we ate some old frozen pizza from the freezer. There's no graceful way to reenter normal life and get back into the routine.

In some ways, it felt like the real summer was beginning now. There were still more than six weeks of summer left, and I had no idea how I was going to get through them. The momentum of '50s fun had slowed, our beach week—the highlight of the summer—had passed, and there was nothing left for me to do but slog through the rest of the summer in a cluttered, dusty home with restless children.

I tried to buck up. Wasn't a bunch of nothing what I had wanted? Hadn't I wanted to slow my life to a crawl?

With nothing to do and nothing to look forward to, I felt lost for a few days. I dragged the kids to ShopRite and let them pick out treats like Yodels or Toaster Strudels—foods I never bought unless they were with me. The kids thought ShopRite was fun, and they danced up and down the aisles grabbing plungers to swordfight, eating way too many cracker samples, and talking with their mouths full. I enjoyed it, in a *What else do I have to do anyway?* kind of style, but mostly I felt exhausted. And I ended up back at the store two days later to buy all the stuff I was too distracted to remember before.

I made the kids clean their room, and I cleaned the fridge. After spending a week with my tidy mother in a spotless rental, my own dis-ordered house depressed me. I fantasized about how it would look if I could have three uninterrupted days to do the whole house. (This is a repeated fantasy I have nurtured for eighteen years.)

Here's what was great about the schedule-free summer: it didn't matter what time we woke up. It didn't matter what time we ate breakfast. I never had to hurry the kids along. They were relaxed and flowed along well with the empty days, bickering notwithstanding. When we did errands together, we had interesting, rambling conversations. They fiddled around the house. They would go upstairs to make their beds and end up designing a new spaceship out of Legos. They might sit for a half an hour picking out a tune on the piano. We were moving really slowly, which was my goal, but it still felt weird. Days passed with nothing more than errands, housework, and random play.

Here's what I didn't like: they watched so much TV. Let me rephrase that: it's not that I didn't like it; it's that I felt guilty about it. Should I be turning off the TV and forcing them to play without it? After all, in the 1950s, there was no programming for children during the day. They had *Captain Kangaroo*, but I think that was over by nine o'clock a.m. And I had figured that this relaxed summer would be healthy for my kids, but instead they were just frying their brains on Cartoon Network. Everyone knows if a kid watches more than a couple of hours of boob tube a day, it's a grave moral fault on the part of the parents. All that TV puts them at higher risk for obesity, stupidity, and failure.

Then one day at around noon, I realized the TV wasn't on. They had turned off the TV without being asked. They had Legos spread out all over the living room. They were chattering and creating. I had been writing for two hours completely uninterrupted. I couldn't believe it. This was exactly what I had hoped for when I imagined the summer. Bliss.

Around lunchtime, Sam came in, looking for a Lego piece. "So, Mom," he said, "we're just having a relaxing, stay-at-home day?"

"Yes," I replied.

"Yay!" he said. He was still in his pajamas, and it was one o'clock in the afternoon.

Sweet Boredom

Summer vacation is a relatively new trend in the history of mankind. It's only about one hundred years old. For most people of the past, school was an irregular proposition at best, so vacation from school was unnecessary. During the 1800s, rural kids went to school in the summer and winter so that they could have the spring and fall off to help with planting and harvesting. But for every American alive today, summer vacation is sacred. We all believe deeply in the restorative power of long, lazy afternoons, burgers on the grill, and days at the beach. Even as adults, before we had children, my husband and I celebrated the beginning of summer by spending Memorial Day at a friend's weekend place by a pool or a lake. Often that meant shivering under a towel because the temperature never got above seventy-two degrees; nonetheless, we viewed our first summer weekend as an important rite of passage each year. Summer promises rejuvenation. And even before the kids came, we needed that.

When I remember my own childhood summers, the one thing that stands out is the boredom. Not the restless boredom that comes from sitting in science class with the teacher droning on and on or the trapped boredom of sitting at the dinner table while your parents talk about insurance and don't allow you to be excused. No, I mean the sweet boredom that comes from the total absence of necessary activity. It means you lie on the glider on the screened porch and stare at the pine-knot ceiling, trying to pick out faces in the wood. It means you and your friends drape yourselves over the living room sofas, asking each other over and over again "What shall we do?" and then systematically rejecting every idea that comes along. The sofas are itchy, and it's a little hot, but still you don't go outside. You're too lazy. Then you get the giggles when someone unexpectedly burps, and you giggle for half an hour until finally your friends have to go home.

I don't remember my parents engineering constant stimulation for us. We had choices: we could ride our bikes; we could play in the sprinklers; we could lie on the itchy sofas and whine. And we often chose to lie around and whine. It felt good.

One morning, I was trying to get us out of the house to do an errand. I turned off the TV and sent the kids upstairs to get dressed and make their beds. An hour later, I hadn't heard from them. I shouted upstairs to Jack.

Me: "What are you doing?"

Jack: "Um, well . . . "

Me: "Did you make your bed?"

Jack: "Well, no . . . I was going to make my bed, but then there were Legos on it, so I decided to get dressed first, but then I couldn't decide what to wear, so I just didn't know what to do."

Sweet boredom.

The Evils of Video Games—and Even Worse: Cell Phones

When they were not delighting in boredom, the boys played video games. Not sports games, not educational games . . . no, they played fighting games. In later years, they came to adore Minecraft, but during that summer, Minecraft had not yet been invented, and their favorites by a wide margin were Pokémon, Mario, Sonic the Hedgehog, and Teenage Mutant Ninja Turtles. Games in which you simply beat the crap out of your opponent. It was the only type of game they liked. I was embarrassed about this because many of their friends played "enriching" games where you built cities or, at the very least, sports games where you sort of learn about sports stuff. But my kids just wanted cartoon violence, and in my worn-out, pick-your-battles parenting style, I just allowed it. I didn't like it, but I allowed it.

Things that a 1950s mother would say about video games:

- "My, that looks exciting."
- "How do I clean that controller?"
- "Well, that's fine, dear, but put it down now and go outside and play."

One day, Sam had a friend over, and this friend had something much more interesting than a video game. He had a cell phone. At the age of eleven, we had reached the point in growing up where many of his friends had cell phones. The friend was texting, and he and Sam were giggling at it. They blatantly kept it away from Jack as if they had some big secret. I was worried that they were doing something dirty or using swear words.

I know all kids have cell phones these days, but when Sam was eleven, it was still unusual for a fifth grader to have a cell phone. I was not prepared for this new threat to childhood: the texting, the sexting, the bullying. I had known about it but figured it was way off in the future. Now here it was, right in my living room. The friend and his cell phone were telling Sam which girls liked him, and, apparently, there were quite a few. Sam was emboldened. "I'm glad they're coming around!" he declared.

Things that a 1950s mom would say about texting:

- "My, that's a tiny typewriter!"
- "How do I clean that?"
- "Well, that's fine, dear, but put it down now and go outside and play."

I hovered in the other room, feeling confused and unprepared. I knew there should be some rules about his, but I hadn't thought a darn thing through. I had filed *cell phone usage* in my brain under *stuff to think about when they're teens* and was totally adrift. I just occasionally shouted lame things from the kitchen like, "OK, guys, almost done on that thing?" or "You two want to have a snack?" and "Guys, one more minute and you need to put that away."

Eventually, they did stop texting and played a video game. I couldn't believe how relieved I was to see them enjoying cartoon violence.

Take Me Out to the Ballgame

One night, we had tickets for a Jackals game. The Jackals are our local baseball team, and their games are lots of fun. The games always have a theme to them, and they have a silly mascot, and the stadium is small, so all the seats are good. We had gone to a game the year before for Harry Potter Night, and the kids wore their Harry Potter robes and wands. The food was good stadium food: burgers, cheese fries, pizza. I was looking forward to it because I didn't have to cook. Also, the tickets were super cheap, and in fact, two of them were free because Jack had won them in a school contest.

We were not big sports fans, but I knew we'd have fun anyway, and a local ball game sounded to me like a total 1950s experience.

As it came time to leave, though, no one wanted to go. Sam was too tired; Jack admitted he was only going for the food. My husband would rather cut the lawn. Yes, really, he would.

I realized with disgust that I would literally be dragging my entire family through the evening, and I just didn't have the energy for that. So we decided not to go, and I was ticked off. What is wrong with my family? Who doesn't want to go to a relaxed baseball game on a beautiful summer night and eat cheese fries? Were we so tired and inert that we forgot how to have fun?

We stayed home, but I had no food in the house because I didn't think I was cooking. We ended up at the diner, and just as we sat down, Jack flopped over in the booth and whined. He didn't want to sit next to Bill. I asked him why not. "Because he is ANNOYING!" he bleated. Bill didn't hear it, but I was infuriated. What kind of a brat talks like that about his father when he's about to eat out in a restaurant? I yanked Jack up and announced that we were leaving. Bill was confused . . . aren't we eating here?

In the car, I yelled at Jack for being ill-mannered, ungrateful, and disrespectful. I didn't want behavior like that, and I felt sure that no 1950s mother would have put up with it, either. At home, I gave him a quick hot dog and sent him to bed.

Then Bill and Sam headed back to the diner—they had to eat, after all. While driving there, they discussed Sam's tent mate at upcoming Boy Scout camp. The boys were allowed to choose their own tent mates, and Sam had agreed to bunk with the first friend that had asked him. Then, Sam declared, a second friend asked him, so he dumped the first one. He was pleased with his decision and looking forward to camp.

Bill turned the car around and brought Sam home so we could both yell at him. You don't treat friends like that!

To set things right, Bill immediately drove Sam all over town to tell the second friend he would not be able to tent with him after all and then to the first friend's house to say he would be tenting with him and that he was sorry for his behavior. I waited at home. I was starving; it was almost nine o'clock p.m.; there was no food in the house; both my kids were ill-mannered brats. The lawn looked good, though.

Bill and Sam came home, and I fixed Sam a burger from the last frozen patty I had in the freezer. We had no buns, so he had it on wheat toast. Jack was upstairs filled with remorse over his "annoying" comment, Sam was filled with remorse over how he treated his friends, and my husband and I were filled with remorse for the delicious burger and fries we could have been having at the diner. We put everyone to bed and ordered sushi for ourselves, which didn't arrive until ten o'clock.

We should have just gone to the baseball game.

Boredom Is No Longer Sweet

By this time, it was mid-July and Bill had hit upon a busy time at work, so he was gone long hours. I was on my own with the kids for days on end. They were sick of the pool. They didn't want to hit tennis balls. They didn't want to go to the park. They picked on each other just for the heck of it.

I tried hundreds of ways to get us to do something fun. The problem was that we had totally different ideas of what was fun. For me, a fun thing to do would be to go to the library and browse among books and magazines, then check out some stuff and bring it home and read it. They'd rather get a tooth pulled.

I might suggest we head to the mall, because Sam needed socks, and maybe there would be a sale on sheets, which we also needed, and we could have lunch at McDonald's. They paused, deciding. No thanks. The toys in the Happy Meals are too boring.

We could go into the city, I'd say. Maybe meet Dad for lunch. They just stared blankly. "Well, we have to do something!" I said. "We can't just sit around here all day."

"Yes, we can," Jack said. "Besides, we won't just sit around. We'll play video games."

I had to face the fact that the summer wasn't going that well. Although I was less distracted, I was not enjoying myself. The boys seemed so slothful that it disturbed me, which just stressed me out. Meals, cleaning, and all other housewife tasks were interrupted every five minutes with questions, needs, or complaints from the kids.

On a particularly miserable day, I had spent four hours doing paperwork: calling insurance companies, straightening out bills, returning correspondence, and writing thank-you notes. The crushing tedium of it had me exhausted. We couldn't go to the pool because it was going to thunder.

I went upstairs to watch *Oprah*, who at the time was on every day at four o'clock p.m. I desperately needed to hear an adult talk. She had on a bunch of women who were raped or otherwise victimized. It didn't help.

Eventually, we turned the TV off, had dinner, and cleaned up toys. The kids couldn't do anything without torturing each other. "He's going to lick me!" screamed Jack. One minute they were crying and the next they were laughing, like weird, cabin-fever, bipolar monkeys. I tried to turn on the news, but it was just stuff I already knew, and I couldn't hear it anyway over the kids' shrieking.

After dinner, I wanted to stick one of the boys in the bath, but there was lightning outside and you're not supposed to bathe during lightning. I know that everybody in the whole world showers during a lightning storm, but for some reason, I just can't bring myself to do it. I went into the kitchen and ate half a sleeve of Oreos. I really needed to get out of the house. Or read a book. I needed help.

Bill called to say he was still more than an hour away. But—he had a great day at work. Terrific project! Lots of fun! Really fulfilling! Super.

Giant black flies were in the house. I figured we had a hole in some screen. The dog wanted to catch and eat them. He snapped his head around and danced after them, growling. He whipped his head around so fast over and over again that he looked like a psycho. When he caught the flies, he would eat them whole (gross!) or spit them out, wet and mutilated, onto the floor (even grosser!).

FINALLY, at 9:15 p.m., the boys were in their beds, reading. I was ready to relax. Then came a loud thunderstorm. It had been building all day, and it was a doozy. The kids got nervous and wanted flashlights. The dog got nervous and humped my leg. I went from room to room searching for flashlights while the dog humped my leg. I couldn't find any flashlights. Bill was still not home.

Twenty minutes later, I found a flashlight. The batteries were dead. The dog was under a bed.

Bill got home at 10:30 p.m. It was a long drive in that thunderstorm. I didn't want to hear about his day. I just wanted to be alone, because I had realized that the kids were going to wake up at seven o'clock tomorrow morning, and we had no plans or anything to do, so tomorrow would be just like today.

Let's Run

There was a free track program in town for grade-school kids. It met once a week from seven to eight thirty in the evening and was run by coaches from the high school to introduce kids to running, jumping, and other track skills in a fun, low-key way. Many of our friends had done it and raved about it. It was a structured evening with coaches and stated learning goals, so it was in direct contrast to my summer from the 1950s, but I forced the kids to do it anyway, just once, to try it. Their lethargy was starting to alarm me; wasn't there anything they were motivated to do? When I allowed them to do nothing all summer, I just assumed some activities would come to the forefront that they would enjoy. None had. Even if they never ran track in their lives, perhaps they would enjoy this weekly activity from a social standpoint. There was no commitment to attend, and I promised them they wouldn't have to go again if they tried it once.

Many of their favorite friends were there. The kids were broken up by age, and they did all sorts of throwing and running games on the field. When it was over, my boys spontaneously ran extra laps with their friends. They raced each other; they wouldn't come off the field. We were practically the last to leave.

On the way to the car, they were sweaty and laughing, obviously having a ton of fun. I asked, did you like it? No, they answered. They hated it. They didn't ever want to do it again.

Come and Eat!

And then there was dinner. No matter what else happened that day, be it glorious or boring as heck, there still needed to be an evening meal. In the 1950s, getting a wholesome meal on a beautifully set table was practically a religion for mothers. On *Leave it to Beaver*, I had watched Mrs. Cleaver serve her family a soup course as a matter of routine. She even provided a soup spoon, and the family would graze the spoon across the surface of the soup away from their body and then tilt the spoon tidily into their mouths without getting a soup mustache. Yes, the Beaver knew how to eat soup politely, all because June Cleaver went into that kitchen every day at four thirty, put on an apron, and got it done.

I, too, put dinner on the table almost every night because I was committed to our family eating together and because, truthfully, we had some of our best times around the dinner table. We also had some of our most stressful times, because it's a tough time of day for everyone, and the kids' manners could be so atrocious.

Choosing what to cook is just the beginning of dinner difficulties. Certainly, no one today can claim lack of inspiration. There are dozens of food shows on TV to help you along. The cooking shows are supposed to inspire you to try new recipes, and sometimes they do have good ideas. But mostly they're just cooking, and as all of us moms know, getting dinner on the table is not just cooking. Anyone can cook a good meal when all the ingredients are purchased and laid out for them, every utensil or appliance you need is clean and in working order, and no young boys are running through the kitchen with their shirts off yelling, "I arrested you already!"

Here's my idea for a cooking show: *Dinner at Donna's.*

The show starts with Donna, a fit and fun forty-something mom who loves to introduce her family to new recipes. Donna is on her way to the grocery store to buy what she needs for tonight's meal: grilled salmon, potato parsnip puree, and a salad involving Swiss chard. Suddenly, her cell phone rings. It's the school nurse calling; her fifth-grade son, Dylan, has a fever. Donna turns the car around, goes to the school, and brings Dylan straight home to rest. She gives him Children's Advil, and he takes a monster nap. Donna is unable to get to the grocery store. She is almost out of food, so she scrounges around the pantry to see what she could possibly make for dinner. She finds some old fun-size candy bars, which she promptly eats, because stress eating is the best response she can think of.

The next part of the show takes place at five thirty p.m. Danny and Diane are home from school. Donna has decided on tacos, but before she can start dinner, she has to do the breakfast dishes that she never got to. Then she has to clean all the PTO notices, permission slips, and Cub Scout popcorn order forms off her countertop. Next, she picks up all the shoes, hats, and backpacks that the kids have dumped on the kitchen floor.

Now . . . the food. Donna throws some partially thawed ground beef into a pan and sprinkles it with an old seasoning packet she found stuck to a molasses jar next to the aforementioned fun-size candy bars. She sets the meat on the table with tortillas, a jar of salsa, sliced green peppers, and a big bunch of grapes. Donna's husband, Dave, an angel, shows no disappointment that it's the third time this month they've had tacos. The kids' manners are terrible, and no dessert is served.

The finale of the show is clean-up time. The grown-ups chat while the kids clear the table, and it's a miracle nothing gets broken. Dylan is now feeling well enough to chase the dog all over the house. Donna puts all the food away. She wipes off the dining room table, loads the dishwasher, and wipes down the countertops. She washes the pot that won't fit into the dishwasher. She empties the trash. She runs the disposal.

Suddenly she hears the children yelling at her from the living room. She turns the disposal off and goes to see what the matter is.

Nothing is the matter. The dog tilted his head in a cute way and they had to tell her. Donna smiles and suddenly realizes it's getting late and the kids need a bath. She ushers them upstairs, rushes them through a shower, puts each of them in their own beds with a book, and then sends her husband upstairs to read to them.

It is nine o'clock p.m. She returns to the kitchen, finishes running the disposal, starts the dishwasher, and makes the coffee for morning. Dinner is done. The show ends as Donna turns out the lights in the kitchen and pats the dog goodnight.

Donna loves her family, and she's very grateful for her pantry. She knows that someday she will make grilled salmon and potato parsnip puree, and it will be sublime. She also knows that for the luckiest family chefs, tacos are a four-star meal by themselves.

Story Time

I was hoping that the boys would get bored enough this summer to actually read. They didn't. Not that summer and not any other summers. Neither of them were ever readers. Yes, they read well in school, but reading a book for enjoyment is not an activity they chose on their own. Even in high school, they read the bare minimum in English class to get an A. Their dislike of reading bothered me, first, because I love to read and would have enjoyed sharing books with them. Second, parents are constantly reminded how important reading is to overall success in school and business. The fact that my kids hated to read seemed to doom them to mediocrity.

I had planned to require them to read a half hour a day that summer, but the squawking protests that request unleashed defeated me early on. I was yelling and nagging to try to get them to open a book, and that was not what I wanted my 1950s to be about, so I gave up.

In desperation, I tried to at least read to them. I had some success earlier that year with *My Side of the Mountain* by Jean Craighead George. It's the story of a fourteen-year-old boy who runs away from home and literally lives on a mountain by himself: trapping and cooking his own food, living in a hollowed-out tree, etc. He trains a falcon to be his pet. His parents never come looking for him, assuming he can take care of himself. He is free. They loved every page.

So over the summer, I picked *The Phantom Tollbooth* by Norton Juster. A little boy, Milo, sees nothing of interest in the world around him, and then one day, he is transported to a land where everything is different. It's a nonsensical story that makes lots of sense, and since the boys loved puzzles and riddles, I imagined we would love reading this together. But when I read, Sam was bored. He played with Legos while listening but eventually just left the room. Jack tolerated it. I think he was afraid to hurt my feelings.

I tried to tell myself that even though they didn't read, the time they spent building and creating with Legos would strengthen their imaginations enough to keep them from being hopeless illiterates. There were Legos absolutely everywhere: all over the floors, between their sheets, in their pockets, on top of the toilet tank. And the boys constantly created new things—little weapons or spaceships or fighter jets—and they'd come and show them to me. I prayed that somehow this building was just as valuable as reading books. Because really, if somebody asked me what my kids were doing this summer, I'd have to answer: "Sitting on the floor in their pajamas pressing random Lego pieces together."

I was letting the kids do nothing all day, but then when they enjoyed the nothing, I was disappointed in them. I guess I had figured that after a few weeks of slack, their own curiosity and energy would lead them to some exciting new activities. But it hadn't, not one little bit. I had pledged an achievement-free summer, but when it came time to live it, I couldn't trust that it was OK to just relax.

The week before, when we were on vacation, it was easier to be slow. When you're on vacation, you are at your destination. You are not trying to get someplace else—you are where you want to be. You have a finite time at that destination and no goals other than to enjoy yourself in the ways you planned.

Family life in the 1950s was like this. The women got married and had kids. That was their goal. Once marriage and kids were checked off, they had arrived at their destination and then spent their time exploring and enjoying it.

These days, family life is constant striving. Getting married and having kids is not the goal; it's just the beginning. Then you need a bigger house with a fancier kitchen, and your kids need to be improved and enriched, not simply raised. You are not at a destination you can enjoy. You are in constant forward motion with more to accomplish and no time to relax.

In my own life, I was overly concerned with accomplishments and order. I wanted certain things; I had my goals and believed that was the way to happiness. (Even though I knew that "happiness is a journey, not a destination." I had a poster with those exact words hanging in my room growing up.) Still, I found it almost impossible to live that way. My grandmother lived to be ninety-six. She raised her kids during the Depression, and her oldest son was killed in World War II. She saw many, many hardships in her life. She always said to me, "Ambition is fine, but it's not the same as happiness." Could I live that way? Could I raise my children to believe it? Should I?

i quit

Living Colors were made for women in love. They radiate the fire on her lips that burns deep in her heart.

—Tangee Lipstick ad, 1955

Good morning, Mrs. Cleaver. That's a very pretty dress.

—Eddie Haskell,
Leave It to Beaver, "New Neighbors," 1957

I like that T-shirt.

—Bill, to me, hoping the kids go to bed early

Bill continued to be busy at work, and I was holding down the fort, swamped with paperwork, chores, and writing deadlines. The kids were climbing the walls because we'd had some bad weather and didn't go to the pool for a few days. Frankly, the summer had turned into drudgery.

One night, Sam had an evening playdate. A friend had invited him over at seven o'clock for a couple of hours. I said yes because I couldn't think of a good reason not to. But it felt weird and grown up for him to go out at night, and I was aware (again) of how quickly childhood passes.

Later that night at bedtime, I read *The Phantom Tollbooth* with the boys. The chapter had a section about a city called Reality. Reality used to be a beautiful city of lovely homes and parks and plenty of wonderful things to see. But then one day, the residents of Reality realized that if they walked really fast and just looked at their shoes, they got where they wanted to go much faster. They stopped looking at the wonders around them. Gradually, the city, since it wasn't being looked at, began to fade, and finally, it disappeared. Inattention to the joys of life caused them to vanish. My stomach lurched.

I was living in Reality. My kids had slowed down and were enjoying everything. Why wasn't I?

Although I didn't have the stress of dragging the kids through a schedule, I was still dragging myself through one. I walked the dog, did laundry, fed everybody, unloaded the dishwasher, answered the mail, wrote, cleaned up, and wrote some more.

I mentioned all this to my husband, and he just shrugged. He thought my 1950s summer was a nonevent. To him, nothing was different. Where were the crew cuts and the Milton Bradley games? He had given me a cookbook with recipes from the 1950s, a funny old book he'd picked up at a garage sale. I browsed through the pages of kabobs and casseroles made from canned goods, thinking maybe we would try some retro food. I changed my mind when I read the recipes: a typical dish contained cream cheese, condensed cream of mushroom soup, sour cream, mayonnaise, and half and half. Not one or two of those ingredients—all of them.

My kids were not going to eat that. In fact, Bill would never eat that either. Every time I read him a recipe, he said, well, you could use fresh mushrooms instead of canned, or you could use some fresh herbs instead of the Lipton Soup Mix. "BUT THEN IT'S NOT THE FIFTIES," I said.

Bill wished I would throw out the TV, turn the radio to AM, and heat up our coffee on the stove instead of in the microwave. I am certain he wished he would come home to find me in a dress and hose (garters underneath, of course), vacuuming and polishing. Time-traveling back with the family sounded like a blast. Of course it sounded like a blast to him, because he would not be the one wearing a dress and vacuuming. This was the same argument we had had in the beginning of the summer; now it had more bite because I clearly felt like my summer adventure was just a muddle. But manufacturing the fake fifties would be a Herculean effort, and effort was what I was running from. I just wanted to use the 1950s as a prism through which I could view my life in a new way.

His criticism got to me, though, because he was right about this: I was having the 1950s on my own terms. I picked and chose what I wanted from that decade. While I had been willing to give up hothouse parenting, I had not been willing to give up working. Though some mothers of the 1950s worked, most housewives did not, and in fact, the precious image of fifties family life that I had appointed as my holy grail had at its center a woman who had no career at all and no thought of one. She was wholly devoted to home and family.

This was why I could not relax. I spent all my time thinking about work without even realizing it. I woke up every morning and, after I walked the dog, would sit down to write. When I stopped writing, I would spend the rest of the day thinking about when I would write again. I would clip articles or make notes for ideas or squeeze in phone calls. To the casual observer, it didn't look like I was working. But I was working all the time. My head was working all the time.

So, I thought, I could stop. That sounds like a nondecision, because really, I just wrote at home and sold my stuff on a freelance basis, so if I didn't work for a month, no one was going to care. I wasn't a surgeon—no hospital was going to call and beg me to come in to perform some tricky operation on an abscessed appendix. It's not even like any newspaper editors were going to call and say, "Hey, we really miss your crackling brand of humor! Please send us some copy!" No one would miss me if I stopped working.

Earlier in the school year, Jack had to do a writing assignment in which he described each family member with an activity. He wrote: *Daddy tells great jokes, Sam is good at swordfights, and Mommy types on the computer.* Ouch.

I thought of myself as a very hands-on mother, and I thought that I had kept my writing out of the way of my kids' lives. But obviously not. Jack didn't write *Mommy reads good bedtime stories* or *Mommy plays fun games in the pool* or even *Mommy is a good cook.* He said I type.

So I rearranged a few things, and voilà! I stopped working. I even stopped thinking about work. After all, it was only for a month or so; my ego could handle that. I wanted to commit fully to being the doting and mentally available mother. I had the feeling it was the only way to make this summer truly worthwhile.

Quitting work gave me an immediate sense of relief. A burden had been lifted. Things seemed so simple now! All I had to do was keep house, feed the family, and think of fun stuff to do each day. How easy is that?

Officially a SAHM

Not working freed up some mental energy for more reading. I read *The Fifties* by David Halberstam, a thorough journalistic examination of that decade. I read a popular novel from that time, *The Man in the Gray Flannel Suit* by Sloan Wilson, and many magazines from the fifties.

Although some women worked, the ideal married woman did not hold down a job. Having a career made women appear rough and aggressive, and what man would want to marry that? A woman was supposed to be soft, loving, tidy, and completely focused on her husband and children. Everything she did was calculated to support the man's career and keep a home that was welcoming and neat.

The fifties was a time when people kept up appearances. That's why everyone looked so good. When you see an ad for a car in *Life* magazine from 1954, the family is beautifully groomed. The father wears a hat, the mother has a smart handbag and gloves, and the kids wear socks and real shoes—not sneakers. They are smiling and standing in front of a stylish and updated house. It may not be a big house, but it is neat as a pin. Today's ad would feature a mom in yoga pants, a dad who works at home, and kids who are adorably unruly. Compared to the '50s family, we all look like we're wearing pajamas.

At the core of this picture of domestic '50s bliss was the mother. It was she who kept it all running with grace and efficiency. And the moms knew what to do because they had examples to follow from magazines like *McCall's* and *Ladies' Home Journal* and television shows like *Ozzie and Harriet*, *Father Knows Best*, and *Leave it to Beaver*.

I had grown up watching *Father Knows Best* because it was in heavy reruns during the after-school hours. I knew well all the stories of Princess, Bud, and Kathy. I definitely knew how beautiful Margaret Anderson looked in a dress, hose, pumps, and pearls as she warmly sorted out the various troubles of the family. I appreciated the show as a glossy piece of artifice from another time, but women watching the show during the 1950s wanted to emulate her.

The homes in those shows were always tasteful and tidy. Living rooms had coffee tables with flowers on them, not piles of homework, magazines, and dominoes. The children's bedrooms had little writing desks and a single toy box with a lid that actually closed. They had foyers with plenty of room to welcome guests, not piles of recyclables waiting to go out or camping gear that should have been put away two weeks ago.

When her friends dropped in, Margaret Anderson served them coffee in a china cup with a saucer. They took time to sit down at the kitchen table, which had a pretty, ironed tablecloth on it, and chatted while they drank.

Today, we see ourselves as less formal, more real, more in touch with the important things in life. But if we're so much more relaxed, why do we all have acid reflux?

In the 1950s, it was *de rigueur* to hide your stress and put forth a good impression. Today, we let it all hang out. We admit our affinities for Xanax, for therapists, for yoga. But all that admitting doesn't change anything. Though we acknowledge our pressures, we are still powerless against them.

Projects and Field Trips

I started thinking of ways to fix up the house. *I am a smart, hardworking, creative person. I can have a beautiful home, and, darn it, I will have a beautiful home.* My head was filling with domestic fantasies. I could have a pleasing pantry with painted, labeled shelves. I could serve appetizers of homemade breadsticks and herb butter made with chives from my own garden. I saw a project in a magazine where you make a pillow out of a family photo. What a great idea for Christmas presents . . . I could make one for everyone in the family! If I did that over the summer, I could just wrap them up and they'd be ready in December. I would be the perfect housewife if I did that.

I got an instant lift thinking about how rewarding this time would be. I would devote myself to various household projects that had been left undone. High on the list was the photo albums. I wanted to get those done over the summer, because once school started, there would be no time for a project like that. I planned to fix up the spare bedroom, which, at the time, was a ghastly muddle of toys we didn't have the fortitude to throw out. I would make some new curtains for the bedrooms, spruce up the hallway with some adorably framed children's art, and live in such a way that the children's T-shirts would always be folded neatly in their drawers. I would be able to spend more time on the kids and our beautiful home without feeling stressed and torn in two pieces.

In addition, now that I wasn't working, I wanted to go have fun. I made a big list of all the things I wanted to do with the kids: a Broadway show, museums, water parks, movies, etc. I had coupons and discount codes for many of these things, so it wouldn't even cost us a lot of money. I checked the calendar. Five weeks of summer left. Plenty of time. If we did two items on the list each week, we would have an action-packed month of fun.

Of course, I realized that I was now planning and running the risk of enriching (museums!) my children. I was not supposed to plan or enrich. I was just supposed to float. But, come on, didn't '50s moms take their kids to movies? I knew they took them to picnics on the beach—I'd seen the pictures. I just wanted to have fun with my children. *Besides*, I thought, *the kids have done a lot of nothing. Surely they are ready for some stimulation.*

Fired up, I went to find the boys. They were in their room, beds unmade, Legos all over. Sam had his iPod earbuds in and was drumming along on his pillows. "Hey guys," I said, "we're going to go see a 3D movie tomorrow—a big IMAX one—about whales and dolphins. It looks great."

They didn't even look up at me. "Do we have to?" asked Jack.

I love big IMAX documentaries. An outside observer at the movie theater might have thought that I was taking my two boys to see this movie because the kids were nature nuts and loved dolphins. They might have thought that I was so nice and patient to rearrange my schedule so that I could take my kids to a nature movie at eleven a.m. But no, my kids wished they were home with SpongeBob. It was I who, because of my own desires and interests, had dragged them out to take a beautifully photographed journey to another world. As time has gone on, I have dragged them to see movies about the Hubble, the African plains, and beavers. They whined, slumped, and rolled their eyes through each experience. They teased me afterward about the dorky movies. Occasionally, they might grudgingly admit that the movie was "kind of good." Usually, they just bolted out into the mall afterward and wanted to go eat their way through the food court.

So this movie was not to enrich them—it was for my own pleasure. A 1950s mom sometimes made the kids do something that she wanted to do, like go visit loopy Aunt Fanny, and it was up to the kids to be polite and compliant during the visit. That's all I hoped for from my children.

The IMAX movie *Dolphins and Whales 3D* was showing once a day at eleven a.m. This meant we had to get up, get dressed, and get moving in the morning, something we were not used to doing.

The boys dragged their feet. They thought they were being funny. They truly did not want to go to this movie. They'd rather stay home in their pajamas and play with Legos. But since I had stopped writing and cleaning was my only creative outlet, I REALLY needed to get out of the house.

They took a very long time getting ready, and then the drive was longer than I remembered. I thought it was about twenty minutes away, and it really was more like thirty. Add to that the walk from the parked car into the theater with two obnoxiously slow boys, and we missed the movie. We were so late they wouldn't even let us pay and enter. I thought my head was going to explode.

I was surprised at the level of my own fury. In the car on the way home, I let them have it. I think I cursed at them. I may have even said things like, "Is there something wrong with you?!"

If a 1950s mother was infuriated by her children, she would stick to "Oh, dear. I'm so disappointed."

My rage came from the facts that (1) they never do what I tell them in any kind of reasonable time frame, and (2) it was finally my turn to have a little fun and they just couldn't be bothered. They did realize how selfish they'd been, and they were definitely sorry. They were also really sorry that they weren't allowed to play video games for the rest of the day.

The next day, we made the movie in plenty of time. It was good, very slow moving and relaxing. Fin whales have to nudge their newborns to the surface every four minutes around the clock for the first several days of their lives so that they can breathe. Margaret Anderson would have been a good fin whale. I don't know if I would be.

be prepared: sam goes to scout camp

Dad will want to borrow this handy, safe electric saw. Just plug it in. Extra blades and full size patterns included.

—Jig Saw Jr. toy saw ad, 1955

Those are worms. They can't hurt ya, Mom. They died a couple weeks ago.

—Beaver Cleaver,
Leave It To Beaver, "Cleaning Up Beaver," 1958

Mom, where's all our ammo?

—Sam and Jack, ready to play

The movie, just that mere forty-five minutes of something different, gave a little gloss to my week. And the rest of the week was out of the routine, too, because we had something else special to do. We had to get Sam ready for his first week at sleepaway Boy Scout camp.

If there's one thing that is totally stuck in time, it is Boy Scout camp: the merit badges, the tents, the dining hall menu. When my husband saw the camp for the first time, he said, "This is exactly like the camp I went to in the 1970s." When I asked Sam what he was looking forward to most about camp, he answered, "Just being on my own."

The preparations were extensive. There was a big list of stuff to get, and I wanted to make sure I got exactly the right things so that he wouldn't get ostracized by fellow campers and, most importantly, so he wouldn't get eaten by a bear because his shampoo smelled like food. I needn't have worried. He didn't shower all week. ("I swam in the lake, Mom.")

Sam needed mosquito netting and a good flashlight with extra batteries. I pictured him going off in the woods by himself in the middle of the night to find the latrine. I didn't like that picture.

I knew I was doing the right thing for him, though, in letting him go. He was ready for some risk, and it was only fair that he have some. When I was his age, I was doing all kinds of things on my own: riding my bike all over town or walking to the library a mile away by myself. He did very little that was unsupervised.

Before he went to camp, there was an important, coming-of-age topic that Bill needed to discuss with him. No, not sex. That had been addressed already. In our school district, fourth grade was when they started covering the basics, and each year after that, they layered on more information. Bill had been having a series of discussions with Sam about sex and puberty (often accompanied by some highly specific freehand drawings), and he had assured Sam that he could always ask us anything. I felt sure he knew just enough that he wouldn't embarrass himself around any campfire boy talk or be too shocked by anything he heard.

Sex was not the issue. We thought he still believed in Santa Claus.

"Yes, Virginia, There Is a Santa Claus."

Kids believe in Santa Claus for way too long these days. I know; it's cute. It's sweet that entire school communities ban together in the Keep the Kids Believing Conspiracy. At first, I just loved the idea. Gradually, though, it struck me as creepy. It's not the Santa thing, per se; it's just the whole backward value system. We want our kids to believe in Santa until middle school, but we're telling them about sex in fourth grade. So . . . Sam, at the age of eleven, knew that unprotected intercourse could give you HIV, but he still thought a fat man from the North Pole was going to slide down his chimney and bring him toys. That's weird to me.

Obviously, I value a long and sweet childhood—otherwise I would not have chased it with a 1950s summer. But I was wary of what I saw as an infantilization of children.

Bill disagreed with me on this. Vehemently. He himself is the biggest kid there is, and he wanted his boys to believe forever, if possible. I had deferred to his opinions because it was so important to him and because I knew that, eventually, Sam would figure out for himself that Santa is not real.

I can hear Bill decrying me now: "He is SO real! He is in our hearts! Magic does exist!" Well, I agree that magic exists, but not by way of a sleigh and eight tiny reindeer. Bill, however, does believe in the tiny reindeer and is suspicious of anyone who doesn't.

Of course, the real meaning of Christmas is to celebrate the birth of Jesus Christ. We are a Catholic family, and we go to church weekly, but as far as kids go, Christmas is Santa. My kids were happy Jesus had a nice birthday, and they usually tried to live his way of love and forgiveness, but let's face it: Jesus is there for us every day, and Santa comes only once a year.

The year before, when Sam was ten, we were reading *Superfudge* by Judy Blume. The *Fudge* series was one of our favorites, and they are some of the funniest and most realistic books I have ever read. We were laughing and enjoying the book, and for some reason, I glanced ahead a few chapters. My eyes landed on a few key words, and I quickly ascertained that trouble lay ahead. The characters had a very frank discussion about Santa Claus, in which it was clear that there was no such thing as Santa and that the gifts come from your parents. I panicked.

We finished the chapter we were reading, and when Sam was in bed, I told Bill about it. After a brief discussion, he got the book, took out a razor blade, and excised the chapter completely. Sam never noticed the difference.

That tells you how deeply committed to Santa Claus my husband is. Nevertheless, he did agree that we didn't want Sam going off to Boy Scout camp and getting teased because he believed in Santa.

Bill planned his talk carefully. He knew exactly what he was going to say so that Sam would not be too crestfallen. He wanted Sam to know that while the man in the red suit may not exactly come down our chimney, gifts would appear, love would surround us, and magic would be created. This is what I love about Bill; when he is passionate about something, he cuts no corners.

Off they went to the diner. They shared some food and talked. We were pretty sure that Sam had doubts already about the existence of Santa Claus, so this talk was more about confirming his doubts while helping him to still believe in the spirit of Christmas, not sharply ending his belief in Santa. Bill had gone so far as to print the famous letter, "Yes, Virginia, there is a Santa Claus," but as he started to read it, he choked up so much that he couldn't get through it. He put it aside and soldiered on. He talked about faith and magic and how even if you can't see or touch something, it can be real. It's like love—you can't see or touch love, but when you feel it in your heart strongly, you just know it's real.

When he was done, Sam stared at him. Then he said, "You're not trying to tell me there's no Santa, are you?"

Bill was shocked. We totally misjudged this—Sam still utterly believed or, at least, he wanted to. This was the key, the *wanting* to believe.

Years later, when Jack was in fifth grade and Sam was a worldly eighth grader, he kept pressuring and teasing Jack. "You know about Santa, right, Jack?" Jack would say, yes, sure, of course, and go along with Sam's taunts in a vague manner. But I couldn't figure out if Jack still believed or not, and Sam, in typical older-brother fashion, couldn't resist bringing it to a head. One evening, he simply blurted out that Santa didn't exist and that the gifts came from your parents. Jack looked at me, unsure if he should believe Sam. I confirmed that yes, what Sam said was true. Jack seemed very well adjusted about it all. He even admitted that he had kind of known for a year or so that there was no such thing as Santa. I was actually relieved because now we could talk openly in the house and not have to wonder or speak in code around Jack. We ended up laughing about it, and Sam, who was always fooling around on his guitar, composed a brief and funny little song titled "No Santa."

But two days later, I was alone in the kitchen with Jack when I suddenly became aware that he was blinking back hot tears. "Jack, what is it?" I asked.

He answered, "Do you remember that thing we talked about the other night? About Christmas and Santa?"

I said, "Yes, of course I do."

"Can we pretend we never had that conversation?" he asked.

"Of course we can," I said. He wanted to still believe, even if he knew he was supposed to be too old to believe. I hugged him, and he felt better instantly, knowing that he could feel about Christmas as he always had.

This was one of my boys' best qualities; they were in no hurry to grow up. Going back to that day at the diner, Bill decided he was not going to be the one to burst Sam's bubble. He did some frantic backpedaling and changed the subject, they finished dinner, and Sam returned home still a believer.

We just had to hope the subject of Santa would not come up at camp.

Shall We Stuff a Mouse?

In addition to the shopping and failed myth debunking, we had one other task. The scouts signed up for various merit badge classes and, when appropriate, would do advance work on them. Sam was taking Mammal Studies, and to this end, we went into Manhattan to the Museum of Natural History so Sam could learn how species are catalogued for his Mammal Studies badge.

The Mammal Studies booklet, which obviously had not been revised in decades, told a scout how to skin and stuff a mouse. You need to make sure the skull has been thoroughly cleansed of the eyes, tongue, and brains. This is not a required activity to earn the badge, just something fun and interesting the scout might want to know about. If you wish to skin and stuff a mouse yourself and you cannot find a suitable dead mouse lying around, you can get a live one, and then you are advised to "talk to your counselor about the best way to exterminate it." (Does PETA know about this?)

After throwing out the mouse project, we headed to the Museum of Natural History and found the children's exhibition hall. It was a fantastic two-story room that had all kinds of things to touch and see up close: live fish, lizards in cages, bones, insects, etc. You can even look through a microscope at cells. It is exactly the type of place you would think a young Boy Scout would love. I could tell Sam was bored, though.

A museum guide sat with Sam and talked to him for twenty minutes about how things are categorized, showing him little drawers and files and lists. They looked at different rocks and fossils. He was allowed to touch various little bones and feathers. I kept Jack busy with some puzzles and watched Sam out of the corner of my eye. He was fidgety, restless, and clearly wanted to leave. He was probably thinking about SpongeBob. The guide had to remind him to pay attention a couple of times.

When it was all over, the kids and I walked around the museum. They walked slowly, staring at their feet instead of the saber-toothed tiger, constantly looking for benches where they could sit down. They were just suffering in silence until they could finally get home and go to the pool. It burned me to realize I had the only boys on the planet who could not appreciate a trip to the Natural History Museum and were singularly unimpressed by grizzly bear dioramas and giant dinosaur bones.

We drove Sam up to camp on the appointed Sunday. At the site, things looked good if you liked rustic. Sam did. His little tent was sagging, patched, and perfectly sized for two boys. He impressed me by shoring up his tent with various knots I couldn't identify. I was pretty sure he was going to have a great week. We stood around while he unpacked and set up.

When I was almost ready to leave Sam and go home, one of the leaders called the boys together and made a bathroom/cleanliness speech. It was more than a mother wants to hear. He emphasized that it was fine, often preferable, to just pee on a tree. No need to find a latrine unless you needed, as he put it, "to take a dump." Now I was definitely ready to leave Sam and go home.

The scouts all headed off to take their swim test. Sam hugged me and kissed me good-bye. He was not embarrassed to hug in front of other scouts, but he was definitely ready for me to leave.

Jack and I returned home together. Bill was a Scout Leader, so he stayed up for a few nights to help out. Back at home, Jack and I walked the dog. The house was so quiet with just the two of us. It felt nice and slow. We ordered pizza and watched a movie. I let him sleep in the big bed with me.

Time for That Domestic Makeover

Without Sam home, the days with Jack were simple. He was an easy child when he was alone; he kept himself happy. I was looking forward to my week with him as a meandering, pressure-free time for the two of us to be together. And I was looking forward to the week as a time when I would kick my domestic makeover into action.

To help inspire me, my latest book was *The Pocket Book of Household Hints* by Holly Cantus, published in 1959. It is a collection of 1,500 tips from readers: "time-saving, tension-saving, money-saving ideas" culled from four million submissions to Mrs. Homemaker's Forum.

Mrs. Homemaker's Forum was a nonprofit organization that served as an exchange for the latest and best methods of housekeeping. If it existed today, it would be a dynamic website.

The foreword to the book goes, in part:

> The American homemaker is a wonderful and versatile person. She does not mind that her world demands that she have many heads; she merely regrets that she has not been given more hands. To be worth her salt the American woman must be a loving wife, devoted mother, active community worker, gardener, seamstress, tutor, economic manager, dietician, cook, laundress, chauffeur and entertaining hostess. . . . She is driven by a desire to improve herself, her home, her town. In her spare time she takes adult education courses or returns to college in order to learn how to be a better bridge player, a better French conversationalist, a better upholsterer of her own furniture, a better participant in political parties.

In her spare time? She had spare time?

That introduction is both funny and intimidating. What was I setting myself up for? I read on, spellbound by the hints offered:

> Windows will stay cleaner if you vacuum your screens frequently.

> Wash and air the clothes hampers frequently, especially in hot weather. Use Pine-Sol to disinfect and deodorize.

Veils, ribbons, lace, ties, even a hem, can be ironed on a light bulb. Remove the shade from the lamp, turn on the light and slowly move the article across the hot bulb.

The American homemaker wants everything in her house attractive. Even a small detail like the rod in the clothes closet does not go unnoticed by the home decorator. Using the adhesive plastic paper offered on the market by several companies, she covers the rod in a color or design to complement her color scheme. When the shoe boxes and hatboxes are covered with the same durable paper, she can be justly proud of her co-ordinated closet.

I guess I really needed to rethink how much stress I was actually under. They cared about their closet rods?

Of course, these tips are no real indication of how actual housewives lived. There is no data to tell us what percentage of women decorated their clothing rods in a complementary manner to their hatboxes. However, the scope and type of tips in this book clearly suggest that there was a social pressure to elevate housekeeping into some sort of Olympic-level competition. If homemaking was the only, or at least the most important, venue for a woman's energies, then perhaps trivial tasks were blown out of proportion into some soulful transcendence that is essential to the happiness and well-being of her family and herself.

To clean decorative stuffed birds, rub gently with a slice of bread. The absorbent bread will pick up all dust and cobwebs without harming the feathers.

I recognized myself in the household hints. Not that I disinfected my clothes hampers; I did not. But the distraction this type of housework provides, the astonishing way in which the trivial business of the day becomes more important than anything else—isn't this the way we all live now? In addition to any housework pressures we may feel, we are caught up in dozens of emails, errands, and information, worried about our children's progress, to the point that we often feel we are too busy to enjoy the day as it passes.

> Paste a diagram of your food-freezer contents on the inside of the freezer top or door. If you add and subtract items as purchased and used, you will have an up-to-date inventory, as well as a guide showing where the various items are stored. If you add the dates of purchase, you will know which items should be used first.

Fired up by those 1,500 household hints, I was primed to get the house in order. I wanted my housekeeping, like my mothering, to experience a sea change this summer, and this was the week to get it started.

> Nylon stockings do a wonderful job of straining used fat. Cut the stockings into round pieces 2 in. larger than mason jars. Fasten to top of jar with elastic bands.

Since Jack had no brother to play with that week, he wanted to play with me. We played, but I also invited him to help me with chores.

> Wash your large powder puffs and give them to the children to use in shining their shoes. The ribbon across the back of the puff will provide a good grip for tiny fingers.

We hosed off the patio chairs and dusted the TV. Without work to distract me, I realized with a shock how slovenly the house was. I tried to clean out some rooms, organize cabinets, or replant dead sections of the garden. The change was slow, but I was determined. I wanted to become someone who grew fresh herbs on her windowsill and put a dried hydrangea arrangement in her fireplace during the summer. At the very least, I wanted to be a woman whose powder room was always presentable, someone who didn't have to shove the clutter out of the way just so an impromptu guest could sit down on the sofa.

> Moist wallpaper cleaner will freshen the texture of book bindings. Paper, cloth or leather bindings can be rubbed with this cleaner, which will also whiten the edges of the pages.

One day that week, we had a friend and her two-year-old visit and come to the pool. This was something I never would have taken the time for if I was still working, so it felt special. I felt sweet and hostessy, entertaining during what would normally have been business hours for me. The girl, Agnes, was adorable, and Jack loved playing with her. We had a great time, but I had forgotten how tiring it was to follow a toddler around. We went to the pool from ten o'clock to almost two o'clock, and I was exhausted. After they left, I fell into a stupor and then a nap. Jack and I went back to the pool for pizza night. It was our fourth time having pizza in a week.

The next day, I tackled the spare bedroom, which we had been calling the playroom since we needed a place for all the extra toys. In reality, it was so crowded a kid couldn't play in there if he'd wanted to; it was just a repository for all the stuff we didn't know what do with. I worked for three hours, organizing, throwing stuff away, dusting and vacuuming. I don't know what I had expected, but the room still looked like a repository. It was still cluttered, the shades were still torn, the furniture was still mismatched and leftover. I couldn't even turn it into an *attractive* repository. It was shattering to realize how much work it would take to get the house in the kind of shape I was envisioning. I had let things slide for way too long. I was a horrible housewife.

> Toothpaste rubbed on the glass tops of furniture or on the glass screen of the TV set is helpful in removing small scratches. Polish with a soft cloth.

The pilot light went out on the water heater, and when the repair guy came to fix it, he suggested that I vacuum around it once in a while. Apparently, it was so thick with dust it was a fire hazard. Now the water heater guy knew I was horrible housewife. After he left, I decided to clean out the basement, which at that time was a big, unfinished mess.

Our house was built in the 1920s, and the dark old basement had an uneven concrete floor, exposed pipes and wires, and rusted little windows that didn't open anymore. We had hung a huge clothesline that stretched across the whole room and snagged your forehead as you walked to the washer. Everywhere there were stacks of dusty boxes filled with who-knows-what and odd pieces of furniture we didn't use but thought we might want to one day. (That day never came. The furniture all ended up at the curb.) I let Jack come down to help me clean. "You're right, Mom," he said. "This is a dump." Now even Jack knew I was a horrible housewife.

> Place a window shade upside down behind the stove. When you cook, pull the shade up and hook it on a small nail in the wall. When you have finished frying the spattering foods, drop the shade down into place and out of sight.

It saddened me to realize that I would have been a tremendous failure as a 1950s housewife. The image that I had been holding so dear during those many months was totally beyond my grasp. I went back to the fifties because it seemed easy: let the kids do nothing, keep a neat house, wear lipstick every day. It seemed uncomplicated, even fun. I wanted to feel good about womanhood, and since I didn't feel good about it in the present day, I thought I would try the 1950s version.

Teddy Bears and Life

The week was about half over when I saw a mom I knew at the library, and we chatted. I told her all about Sam at camp. I was feeling great about the situation. One of the nights, Sam had used a leader's cell phone to call me; he was homesick. But besides that, he hadn't called, so I knew he was having fun and enjoying new freedoms and responsibilities. I had a peaceful feeling. I was so happy with him—and myself—for just surviving being separated for a whole week.

While I was still basking in that beatific glow, my husband called from work. Bill had left the camp for a couple of days to go back to work, and a counselor had called him to tell him that, apparently, Sam had brought a teddy bear to camp. He had been hiding it in his trunk, but some older boys got wind of it, snuck into his tent, dug through his stuff, and strung the bear up in the middle of the campsite. The whole troop knew about it, and Sam was a laughingstock. He was furious and embarrassed, and the kids who did it were getting in big trouble, which made Sam feel even more embarrassed. Good-bye, peaceful feeling.

I had seen the teddy bear sitting out when Sam was packing, but I didn't think he was going to put it in his trunk. I did not go through his luggage, because Boy Scouts are supposed to be more independent than that and 1950s mothers are supposed to let them.

We had told Sam about sex, and we had tried to tell him about Santa, but we never told him, "Don't bring a teddy bear to Boy Scout camp." Perfect.

As far as growing-up experiences, this was a big one. Sam was just being himself, and he made an unfortunate choice, and he had to deal with the pain and consequences. Since it all happened up at camp, there wasn't a lot we could do for Sam. The leaders dealt with it, and Sam just had to cope with the fallout. A couple of scouts stood up for him, several more teased him, and most kept their distance. He found out who his real friends were, and he found out who would rather keep their head down than take a stand on his behalf. All good life lessons. I had checked the list twice, sent Sam off carefully, and thought he was well-prepared for camp. In the many years since then, I have learned that there is always a way for things to go wrong. Preparation is important, but you can't prepare for everything. As the kids have made their way through camps, middle school, play auditions, cliques, high school, inappropriate Facebook posts, and many other things, I have learned that there is always a painful life lesson looming.

Sam and Jack have inevitably had bad things happen to them that any adult would have seen coming and been able to forestall. I would get frustrated or anxious and think, *What is wrong with my kids? When are things going to stop getting so fouled up and run smoothly?* The answer, of course, is that bad things often happen amidst the good.

I had been operating under the assumption that if I did everything right, the kids would be *finished* when they went off to college and wouldn't need me anymore. Ha! My parents saw me through many crises in college: "I want to change my major!", my car dying on the Golden Gate bridge and then again in Las Vegas, cross-country moves, more than a couple of health scares, and a long parade of weird haircuts. They helped me move into a truly appalling neighborhood in New York City, because that's what I could afford; they were nice to all the boyfriends I brought home; they helped me buy my co-op in Manhattan. They were there for the wedding, the newborns, the miscarriage, the first house purchase, and the standard stream of career disappointments. Upheaval is a part of life. Letting go and allowing my children their own journey started that summer, and it is still filled with anxiety for me. Now, though, I try to remember that when my kids make mistakes, it doesn't mean there's something wrong with them—it means they're human.

occupation: housewife

Arise, floor cleaning slaves . . . discover the wonder of vinyl beauty underfoot.

—Flor-Ever ad, 1955

I don't think I could bring myself to leave my garbage disposal.

—June Cleaver,
Leave It to Beaver, "Tenting Tonight," 1958

Mom, there's smoke coming out of the toaster oven!

—Sam

I have to admit, I started to enjoy the summer a little bit more. With just Jack to care for, that week was more relaxed, and no pressure from writing deadlines felt heavenly. I devoted my evenings to charming, homey tasks like mending an old stuffed bunny from my childhood (Fluffy: the one Aunt Virginia peed on in our youth). And I planned a splashy return from Boy Scout camp for Sam. I assumed that after a whole week away from home, living in the "wilderness," he would appreciate being welcomed into an orderly and adorable home with an array of all of his favorite foods at a fun and warm family reunion dinner. This was an idiotic assumption. He was an eleven-year-old boy. He didn't even care if his towel was clean.

It was beautiful weather, so I cleaned off the patio and dragged all kinds of area rugs, cushions, and tablecloths out there. Jack helped me. He kept saying things like, "Are you sure we're supposed to put this rug OUTSIDE?"

I put fresh flowers around. It looked like an outdoor living room, just like what you would see in the magazines. I planned for a delicious splurge of shrimp, Sam's favorite, and sausage on the grill. I was reveling in making the day a delight. I pictured us sitting around feeling extra loving and comfy in the inviting outdoor room, sharing camp stories, laughing, and having lots of eye contact. Everyone would marvel at the lovely oasis I'd created and want to spend time on it, together.

Bill and Sam arrived home from camp. I could not stop staring at Sam. I hadn't laid eyes on him in a week. I hugged him for the longest time, and he hugged me back just as hard. Neither of us wanted to let go. I knew that he was going to leave me, little by little, and join the rest of the world. I could live with that if he was doing well, if he was loving the world and his place in it. And I determined that during the camp week, he did love it. He even rose above the teddy bear fracas and had a wonderful time. I felt like a good mother; I was able to let go and not control so much.

Then I took everyone outside to show them the patio. They didn't think it was inviting; they thought it was weird. Bill actually hated it. He tried to pretend otherwise, because he could see that I'd worked very hard, but it was too out of left field for him. He had not read enough women's magazines to understand why it would be fun to have a rug outside. He was visibly rattled that the round outdoor dining table, which was ALWAYS IN THE MIDDLE OF THE PATIO, had been moved off to the side to make room for other seating. I could tell he was thinking *How are we all going to fit around that table now?* Mostly, he was upset because he wanted to water the lawn and he couldn't do it while there was a rug or a cushion near the edge of the patio. He was forced to hold off on the watering. I think I saw him break a sweat.

Sam didn't know where to sit. The patio was too different for him to relax on. Bill didn't want to sit either; he was busy wandering around the lawn and worrying about the brown spots. He probably thought I had been willfully letting the dog pee all over the lawn every day.

So we perched awkwardly on the patio, and nobody talked. We all kept waiting for Sam to bubble over with hilarious camp stories, but he was too tired. He had worked hard all day on merit badges, jumped like crazy on the water trampoline in the lake, and stayed up late in his tent playing cards. He was wiped out. He simply replied to our questions with one-word answers and stared off in the distance. Jack's feelings were hurt because he missed Sam so much and now Sam was basically ignoring him. Bill went back and forth between reprimanding Sam for his rude, one-word answers and staring at the sprinkler.

Jack just wanted to play with Sam since he hadn't seen him in so long, and Sam just wanted to watch TV since he hadn't done that in a week, and Bill just wanted to set up the sprinkler and then go on the computer to catch up on news and emails. After a forced thirty minutes on the patio, we all went inside to go our separate ways.

Sam took a shower and later a long bath; he was so dirty he needed two passes to get clean. No one cared about dinner. Bill actually didn't even want to grill. I couldn't tell if that was because he was tired or because he hated the patio so much he didn't even want to be on it until I put it back the way it was. I ended up getting take-out tacos, which we ate on the patio—HOORAY FOR ME! And then we all went to bed. I hated everybody.

The next day, we went to church. At home afterward, Bill was not feeling well. He was so tense. There was a lot going on at work, and he just took a few days off to be up at camp as a leader, which put even more pressure on him. He started to have chest pains.

We were both pretty sure he was fine. Still, we worried, and the more we worried, the tighter his chest felt. He started to sweat. I was pretty sure he was fine. I had had similar experiences. It's stress. We are way too stressed. One time when we were on a family vacation to Philadelphia, I became so stressed out I was sure I was dying. I didn't have chest pains, but I was dizzy and I thought my skin might melt. We had to pull off the road to go into a CVS so I could take my blood pressure in one of those free machines. It was 110 over 70. Nothing was wrong with me.

But the stress is endless, and that summer was the summer of 2008, after all, and the economy was tanking. Our money was tight, and I wasn't working. Stuff around the house was broken or disorganized, and we could never get to it. Bill often didn't get home until seven or eight o'clock during the week, and the weekends were full of chores. Time-consuming Cub Scout meetings were about to start for him again in the fall. He never got to unwind.

We were both pretty sure he was not having a heart attack. He should just relax and stop reading about heart attack symptoms on the Internet. But he couldn't relax because I kept staring at him and asking, "Do you feel better now? How about now?" I asked him if he wanted me to call 9-1-1. He didn't.

Sam and Jack had enjoyed about three hours of happy reuniting play, and then the bickering kicked in at an Olympic level. Was it autumn yet? Summers are way too long. Help.

So while Bill worried and the kids fought, I did some laundry. I made lunch. Finally, we drove Bill to the ER.

I was glad he was going because I didn't think he was having a heart attack but the only way we would know for sure was if a doctor said so. Also, in case he really did need treatment for some condition, he would get it. Like, if they had a pill you could take that would turn your children into docile, quiet darlings while you fixed the doorbell and hung five pictures, then he would get that.

I was actually jealous that Bill was going off to enjoy a relaxing EKG while I was stuck at home with the sole responsibility for two bored, bickering, really loud boys. He would get to lie down and watch TV. He could nap. People were going to ask him if he was thirsty. I wished I had chest pains.

I had cleaned all week, but the house still had a long way to go, and now the contents of Sam's and Bill's duffel bags had been emptied and there was damp, pond-smelling stuff piled up in the front hall and living room. The patio still looked darling, but no one wanted to go out there. I needed to go to ShopRite, because even though I had bought some nice things for the special dinner we never had, I had not done my weekly shop. I had been waiting for Bill to come back from camp so that I could leave the boys home with him and get it done by myself. But the big shop couldn't wait another day, and Bill would probably be in the ER for a few hours, so I had to take both boys with me to the grocery store.

They wandered and tripped and fiddled through every aisle. They shouted at each other or laughed too loud at a funny food label. People stared. I saw a man I knew from church; when he heard my kids bellowing about donuts, he froze briefly and managed a fake smile. Whatever.

Bill came home. He was not having a heart attack. He didn't even have elevated blood pressure. He was the picture of health. The doctor suggested he try to relax.

We ate dinner—the shrimp and sausage that I had planned for the night before. Nobody liked it.

I really needed some time alone. I needed to get out. It had been just me and the kids since school had ended. That was OK in the beginning because they were in a summer stupor of inertia. But now they were restless. They were never happy or quiet. When I cleaned out a room or made a nice dinner, nobody cared. Why bother? Did 1950s families appreciate it when mom cleaned the venetian blind cords with white shoe polish?

Just in time, we had a short trip coming up to distract us. We were driving up to visit friends in Maine. I had never been there and was really looking forward to it. I had plenty to do to get ready: Sam had to go to the doctor for an infected bug bite he got at camp, and then, of course, I had to cancel the newspapers, cancel the mail, pay bills, do the laundry from camp, do laundry to get ready to travel, pack, board the dog, and take the kids to the pool every day so they didn't kill each other. No biggie.

The next day, Bill was off from work, which made things easier. We cleaned out the dryer hose. He cleaned out the garage.

> To keep the windshield clear during a hard rainstorm, rub a cheesecloth bag filled with the crushed ends of cigars or any kind of tobacco over the glass. The bag can be kept in one of the compartments of your car.

I went to the gym. I cleaned out another small section of the basement. I took the kids to the park for an hour, but everyone is always out of town in August, so there were no friends to hook up with and they just ended up riding their bikes around with each other. It was kind of a bust.

> When your small children go out to play, tie an old alarm clock on the bike or wagon and set the alarm for the time you wish them to come home.

We rented *Harry Potter and the Sorcerer's Stone* since Jack and Bill had just finished reading it together. We were supposed to watch it at four thirty, but everything got pushed back, as it always does. So we ate hamburgers while we watched it at seven o'clock, and they didn't go to bed till ten o'clock, and I never got to go out and do the two errands after dinner that I had wanted to do.

The next day, I moved all the furniture because the carpet cleaner was coming, and I was hoping the gutter guy would show up, and I made a list of all the things to do to get ready for Maine. I might have been starting to miss working.

We went to the doctor, and on the way there, we stopped at all the houses of Jack's friends to drop off the invitations for his birthday party, which was planned for the week after we returned from Maine. It felt homey and personal to drop the invitations off in person, but it really just meant that I was late getting them out and didn't want the mail to delay them another couple of days.

Then we went to the bank, and the boys started picking on each other. Sam nudged, Jack hit. Sam nudged more, Jack got whiny. Sam nudged more, and finally Jack exploded.

At the doctor's, I had Jack wait in the waiting room while Sam was seen. The minute the boys were reunited in the hallway, the roughhousing and bickering began. In the pharmacy, I had to stand like a sentry between them and hold them apart while we waited for the prescriptions to be filled. I could hardly wait to get home and get away from them.

I canceled the mail and newspapers, cleaned the bathroom, did laundry, made the beds, did the breakfast dishes, and walked and fed the dog. It was raining, so no pool. We were stuck inside.

The next day was more of the same. More chores, more bickering, more rain. Desperate, we went to the library. It was packed with rowdy children and twitching mothers. We were all at our wit's end. I had somehow incurred a twelve dollar overdue fine. Instead of mingling with some of the other kids there, my boys fought with each other, rolling on the floor and making hissing and squealing noises. I should have been embarrassed, but I was too fried to care. Other moms must have been as whacked as I was, because nobody even batted an eyelash about it.

Thank goodness I had plans to go out that night. I had some errands to do, so I built in an extra hour for myself to just wander around the mall. Bill said he would be home early.

That afternoon, I read another chapter in *The Phantom Tollbooth*. The kids never liked reading in the middle of the day; to them, reading was for bedtime when mom didn't let them watch TV anyway. But I insisted, because we desperately needed something to do, and since I was going out at night, I wouldn't be able to read to them later.

In the chapter, the heroes meet a bunch of evildoers, among them "the Terrible Trivium, demon of petty tasks and worthless jobs, ogre of wasted effort, monster of habit." He gets them to move a pile of sand grain by grain, empty a well with an eye dropper, and dig a hole through a granite wall with a sewing needle. After several hours of working in this way, the heroes realize their tasks are going to take a tremendously long time—like about eight hundred years. When they protest, the Terrible Trivium says to them:

> What could be more important than doing unimportant things? If you stop to do enough of them, you'll never get to where you're going. . . . If you only do the easy and useless jobs, you'll never have to worry about the important ones that are so difficult. You just won't have the time. For there's always something to do to keep you from what you really should be doing. . . .

AAAGH, that's me, I thought. *That's a housewife.*

When reading was done, I separated the boys: one outside and one upstairs, and finally it was quiet. I gave Sam all of his prescribed medicines and then cleaned off the dining room table to get ready for dinner. I also had to put the rooms back in order, since I had moved everything for the carpet cleaners. Bill called. He should be on his way "soon."

I prepared flounder, baked potatoes, and green beans. No one ate much; they didn't like it. Their manners were horrible; Sam had to be sent away twice. Bill was still not home.

I cleared the table, leaving the dishes for Bill, and made a list of tasks he would need to do while I was out, including Sam's medicine instructions. I did this so that I wouldn't have to spend time explaining stuff to him when he got home; I could just shoot out the door.

Then I waited. I called Bill. He was still in traffic. I screeched at him, "I THOUGHT YOU WERE COMING HOME EARLY!"

Furious, I simply stood ready to go by the door. Twenty minutes passed. My insides boiled. I was so desperate to get out that I couldn't even sit down in the living room and read a magazine while I waited. I stood, bitter and stubborn, with my purse on my arm, staring at the door. It was half past seven. The stores closed at nine.

Bill came in, apologetic. He didn't realize I needed to go out so urgently. I couldn't even kiss him hello. I showed him the list and bolted. Then I spent my "night out" buying stuff for Jack's birthday party, a thank-you gift for a friend, and house gifts for our upcoming trip to Maine. There was no time for a leisurely browse through the mall.

I was done so quickly, but I couldn't bear to go home. I drove around the neighborhood slowly, block after block, looking at houses. Many were glowing with yellow light from their family rooms or bedrooms. They looked cozy and peaceful. Was that what my house looked like from the outside?

Eventually, I felt like a weirdo driving around looking into windows, so I went home. All the tasks on the list had been done, and everyone was watching the Olympic Games happily. I got on my bathrobe. My night out, my little break, was over.

When we were at the library a few days before, I had checked out *The Feminine Mystique*, the 1963 groundbreaking book by Betty Friedan about unhappy housewives. I saw it sitting on the hall table, but I was too tired to read it.

Bill put the kids in bed. I got on the computer and clicked around the Lands' End Overstock site, looking for something fun to buy that would cost only ten dollars and include free shipping. I kind of felt like shopping, but I was restless, and nothing was fun. I was dreading tomorrow because it was supposed to rain again, I had errands to do, and there were no friends around for the kids to play with.

Suddenly, Jack sneaked up on me. I thought he was in bed. He said he was lonely up there reading in his room. I reminded him that Sam and Dad were also upstairs, so he was not alone. Never mind. He was lonely for me. I opened my arms, and he climbed into our hug, full body to full body, his legs partly wrapped around me, so that as much of us was touching as possible. His head nestled into my neck. I could feel that this hug, this simple act, was cheering him up.

"I'd do anything to make this longer," he said, meaning our hug. And so I shifted my weight so that we were both comfortable and our big hug could turn into a long, talking-time hug.

We talked a little, and I felt so happy and amazed that I could be the source of such enormous comfort. What a gift it is to be a mother and be able to solve problems so easily. At their ages then, if I simply listened to them, or hugged them, or lay down next to them as they fell asleep, their problems vanished. I was the source of their peace and comfort, and I realized how lucky I was to have that job.

We stopped talking. There was no reason to talk or even to move. I smelled Jack's little shampooed head and said a silent prayer of thanks for this sweet, captured moment. This was exactly what I was aching for when I started this 1950s summer. Suddenly, it didn't matter what had happened that day. It didn't matter that I was messy or the boys were wild or that we all got on each other's nerves. It didn't matter because those things don't matter. Jack was in my lap, and we were holding on. The world kept turning at its regular speed, but Jack and I were still.

a tale of two parties

There'll be plenty of action this weekend . . . and you can get it all . . .

—Brownie Movie Camera ad, 1955

What are we having for refreshments?

—Harriet Nelson,
The Adventures of Ozzie and Harriet, "Halloween Party," 1952

Hey, Pammy, it's Friday night!

—My sister Virginia, calling me
from her home in North Carolina so we can talk about our week

Our trip to Maine was splendid. We stopped for lunch on the way up in Kennebunkport. It's a typical quaint Maine town, and we ate lobster rolls for lunch. We even strolled and shopped. It was beautiful and relaxing.

In Belfast, we had a great three days with our friends. We took a sailboat ride, we ate more lobsters, and we strolled and shopped again. I'm pretty sure strolling and shopping is a religion in Maine. Jack was bored with the shopping, but Sam was just reaching the age when browsing in unusual stores was starting to be interesting. It was gratifying for me to experience something with him that we both enjoyed. Throughout most of his life, whenever we did something fun together, it was because I was doing what he wanted to do. I was building a train track with him, I was pretending to be superheroes with him, I was chasing him around the playground . . . you get the idea. I relished those times, because I loved being with my children and watching their imaginations at work. But doing something like window shopping in a quaint Maine town, which I would have enjoyed anyway, well, this was parent/child fun at a whole new level. For the first time, I thought of how delightful it might be to have grown-up children.

The minute we got home, I swung into action planning Jack's birthday party. He had turned eight in April, but we still hadn't had his party because we were too busy last spring to have it. As he has grown up, this hasn't changed. Most years, we have his birthday party during the summer. Jack has always been picky about his friends, and this just increased as he got older. By the time he was in middle school, there would be just a few special ones he wanted to invite. Given everybody's busy schedules, getting those two or three boys together on the same day was practically impossible. Hence, we always have his birthday parties three months late.

It's a Birthday Party—at Last

This year, no prefab bowling parties or karaoke clubs for us; Jack's party was a homemade, old-fashioned, little boy party . . . something right out of the 1950s. We had invited about ten boys to meet us at the park. I had a terrific afternoon of wholesome outdoor games to play. We started the party off with a scavenger hunt then progressed to balloon charades. After that, I had all the boys strap on Nerf vests and play Nerf dart tag. They ran around shooting each other and shouting, falling on the ground "dying," or yelling to each other "Man down! Man down!" It was a gleeful, politically incorrect shoot 'em up, and it was a delight to watch the boys have so much fun without constantly being corrected to *be nice.*

I got a bunch of pizzas delivered to the park, then we had cupcakes instead of birthday cake (no need for forks or plates—I'm a genius!), and then, for the grand finale, I turned them loose with fully loaded water guns. Not little handheld squirt guns; no, these were full-on assault rifles with powerful pump action. They emptied their guns, and I had brought gallons of water so that every kid got one refill. They kept going until they were all soaked to the skin. Jack glowed with pride (or was it the water?) at having such a wild, no-holds-barred birthday party. I felt like the perfect mom.

Now for the Grown-Ups' Turn

For fun, and to satisfy Bill's need for a theme party, we had planned an authentic fifties dinner party. A no-children, dress-up, sit-down-around-a-beautiful-table party. We both love dinner parties, and the 1950s evening promised to be a highlight of our summer. We planned to have hors d'oeuvres on the patio and then a multi-course dinner with a menu from the vintage cookbook that Bill had given me. I cooked everything from scratch. Bill, who loves to cook and usually shares the cooking with me, did not set foot in the kitchen. In his role as a typical

1950s husband, he simply put on the music and grilled the steaks.

Doing all the cooking and prep was more tiring for me but less stressful because the division of labor was clear and I could control my kitchen. Normally, when we entertained, we shared the cooking and we would race around bumping into each other.

There is a refreshing simplicity in the traditional roles. There is no haggling, no confusion about who should be doing what. Each person knows exactly what his or her job is, and they either do it or they don't. These days, the husband and wife each do everything. They both earn money, they both cook, they both change diapers, they both shop for food, and they both take the kids to the pediatrician. It is constant shuffling about, and although the flexibility can be helpful at times, it can also be a muddle. If you have a defined purview, you can say, "OK, the house is clean, and dinner is on the table. I did my job." But if your purview is EVERYTHING, then you are never done, and you end up blaming your husband for not helping more or feeling overwhelmed by the chores you never got to.

Wives have been complaining about sloppy husbands since well before the 1950s, but once women started working full time, figuring out who was going to scrub the stovetop after you both worked all day long became a negotiation. I have to admit, it's not a huge issue in my house because, as I think I've clearly established, I am quite able to ignore a giant mess. But a 1950s housewife would have had different priorities.

I'd been saying I wanted to have a cleaner house, and now I had a huge incentive to clean, because our 1950s dinner party included people that we had never invited over before. I would want to impress these people and may even feel compelled to let them see the whole house—give them the tour, as we say. This meant I had to clean all the bedrooms and the upstairs bathroom.

I started the process Thursday morning to give myself enough time to get through it all without being stressed. Then I got on the phone with my mother, and then she put my father on, too. I talked with my

Dad for a long time. At that point in his Alzheimer's, he still knew and remembered quite a bit. I valued every conversation and stopped worrying about how much time was passing while we talked. I didn't mind idle meandering or repetition; I just enjoyed the rambling. He was still funny, and he remained funny even in his final days. We always laughed a lot.

I did a little cleaning, but then it was time to go to the pool, where we had agreed to meet friends for pizza night. It was perfect weather. I talked with a mom who had high school–aged children. She felt that most kids who get into trouble in high school started to slide in middle school. Her answer was to spend lots of time with her kids during the middle school years: playing games, taking walks, cooking, etc. This comforted me, because I had been thinking that by middle school my kids wouldn't want to do those things with me anymore. It was a relief to know that there were still many years of closeness ahead—that it wouldn't end in grade school.

As it turned out, I have enjoyed wonderful closeness with my boys throughout middle school and most of high school. They needed me more than ever as they faced cliques, bullies, dating, tough teachers, acne, broken bones, summer jobs, and orthodontia. We celebrated the good grades, the successes in plays and band. We traveled and tried new restaurants. We worked on projects around the house. The teen years are scary in so many ways, but what people don't tell you is they can also be wonderful. Embracing my kids for who they really were was a key to navigating the teen years. That kind of acceptance began during the 1950s summer.

Friday, I woke up panicked and thought, "I'm in trouble. I have GOT to clean.

I cleaned, like a maniac, all day long. The boys helped me, sort of, and we took a break in the middle of the day to take the dog to the park. It was a beautiful day, and it was killing me that I had to spend it inside doing housework.

Saturday, I was up early, so excited for our party. Bill had made a mix tape with songs like "How Much Is That Doggy in the Window?" on it. I had expected much more of a *Happy Days* rock-'n'-roll type of sound, but most of the hits were things like "Tennessee Waltz," "Three Coins in a Fountain," and "Tammy." I can see why rock caught on—the Top 40 list was ripe for change.

I printed up our menu on a little card for the guests to see:

MENU

Spam Kabobs
Bacon Cheese Ball with Crackers
Clams Casino
Homemade Chex Mix
Porterhouse Steaks with Horseradish Cream
Succotash
Rice Pilaf
Baked Alaska
Pineapple Upside-Down Cake
Coffee or Tea

I worked all day to make everything from scratch just like a 1950s housewife would have had to do. I made the meringue for the Baked Alaska, spread it over the chocolate cake, and froze it. I made a cheese ball. I made a pineapple upside-down cake. I cleaned up the kitchen, made the kids lunch, made Bill lunch, and then went out to pick up the clams. I made the sauce for the Baked Alaska then went back out to the butcher. The kids helped me vacuum. I took an Advil. I would have taken an aspirin, like a '50s gal, but we didn't have any.

The kids wiped the doggy nose smudges off the glass storm doors. Bill worked in the yard the whole day, like a dervish: mowing, trimming, sweeping, washing patio chairs, etc. I made the horseradish cream, but I didn't chop the onions correctly and it was runny, so I tossed it and made another.

I made a lot from scratch, because really, that's what the women of the 1950s did. Before this summer, I had an image in my head of '50s housewives opening cans of peaches for dessert or delighting in a Betty Crocker cake mix, but in truth, the prepared food industry was still struggling for a foothold in the 1950s.

During World War II, the food industry was revolutionized as the military found new ways to feed their armies on the march. Technology allowed for canned, frozen, and dehydrated meals to taste better than ever, and once the war was over, manufacturers were ready to make money off these tasty new methods. All that was needed was to convince women that these foods were delicious, nutritious, and much easier than traditional cooking.

Thus launched a massive advertising campaign to convince women that they didn't actually like to cook. Wouldn't it be more fun to just open a can?

Women were reluctant at first. They did not believe that opening a can or heating up something frozen was actually cooking, and they were loath to try it. It took years of product testing and marketing before women truly embraced this new "cooking." The 1950s was still a time when most meals were made from scratch.

I find it highly ironic that women today prize cooking from scratch again. People are chopping ginger root and zesting limes and all kinds of labor-intensive activities. I guess working outside the home, micromanaging your children, fundraising for the PTO, and caring for your aging parents isn't enough. We also need to grow our own herbs and shop at six different farmers' markets to find locally grown peaches and kale.

At a time when women are more stressed than ever, do we need entire television networks devoted to the idea that every meal needs to be special, organic, delectable, and arranged attractively on the plate? I don't even understand why people watch these shows . . . are they actually getting recipe ideas that they plan to use or are they simply indulging in wishful fantasies in the way that I would watch a travel show about a river cruise through France?

I showered, set the table, made place cards, made Spam kabobs, put out Chex Mix, fed the kids dinner, sent them outside to play ("But don't mess up the grass!"), and cleaned up their dinner. I was exhausted.

I ran upstairs and got dressed in a sleeveless dress, pearls, and pumps. I donned an apron. I prepped the clams casino for the oven, put the rice on, and set up the coffee. I was still exhausted.

Suddenly, the doorbell rang. The boys shouted, "They're here!" I was dressed, but I didn't have my makeup on yet. Could somebody be early? I wiped my hands and came around the hallway. The front door was open, but nobody was there. The boys laughed. "Just kidding!" they chorused. Bill came tearing in from the patio, and when he saw that no guests were there, he started to laugh. The boys had done it again.

They would play this trick every time we had a party. And we would always fall for it.

Bill showered and put on the music. He looked adorable in his slicked-back hair and vintage bowling shirt, but really, he wears those shirts all the time, so he looked the same as he does every day. He was relaxed and ready to be the perfect 1950s host. Normally, he would be racing around checking his sauce or stirring a gumbo. But since it was the 1950s and the cooking was all my job, he could take it easy. It was fun to see him so relaxed before a party.

The guests arrived, and we had a wonderful time. We even ate the Spam. (It's not bad—just really salty.) People raved over the clams casino, which were surprisingly easy to make, and my cheese ball was delicious. When you mix a bunch of cheese into a ball and then roll it in chopped bacon and nuts, well, that's a home run.

The porterhouse steaks were a revelation. They were so thick we could not stop staring at them. They cost a fortune—four steaks were well over $100—and they were enormous, so each couple shared one. If we hadn't thrown this party, I never would have bought such an outrageously expensive menu item. It was gleefully decadent to enjoy them.

Everything else was delicious, too, even the succotash, which was made from frozen corn and lima beans. The Baked Alaska came out perfectly and was so good. It wasn't that hard, really, just time consuming, so I promised myself I would make it again. (Seven years later, I still haven't.) The whole evening shimmered because we were doing something different. All the little touches Bill and I put in to give it that 1950s feeling, all the extra thought, really paid off as our guests delighted in each detail. The food was such a departure from what we were used to. No one today would serve a homemade cheese ball or Baked Alaska. To eat them in this guise was both scrumptious and fun. The party itself felt grown up—formal and dressed up and planned. It was the kind of thing I had been looking for in the '50s: the feeling that everyday life is enough to celebrate that we don't have to wait for an occasion; each day is worth rejoicing in. We should throw theme parties more often.

The Aftermath

I had thrown two terrific parties in a week: Jack's birthday party and the dinner party. I had packed and unpacked from our long weekend in Maine. I had a hangover of happiness from all the fun we had been having, and I felt fulfilled that my hard work had paid off. Maybe I was not such a bad housewife after all. I was, however, flat on my back with fatigue.

My sciatica was acting up; I had a stiff neck and lower back pain. This could be because I was spending so much time sitting on those flimsy lounge chairs at the swim club. I had a headache almost every day, and my irritable bowel syndrome was giving me stomach cramps. It usually kicks in when I'm stressed or not taking care of myself, which I had basically stopped doing. I was not going to the gym on a regular basis, because it took too much time away from my family.

I felt like I was at the end of a marathon and just wanted to hang on until it was finished. I could see that the summer had been great for the kids. It had been hard on me, but it felt nice to give my kids this gift.

I didn't start out putting everyone first; I had just wanted to give the kids a schedule-free summer. But even with their lack of activities, they still needed me so much. They needed interaction; they needed support; they needed fun. They needed me to take them to friends' houses, and they needed me to have their friends over. They needed to go swimming and learn to ride a bike and to be told that it's time to turn off the TV. They needed to learn to make their beds, to have table manners, to be nice to people, to try new foods, and to cross the street.

When they were at school or camp or a sports practice, someone else was guiding them through all that. When they were at home, it became my job. So when I let my kids stay home and do nothing, I basically signed on for all those teachable moments. I hate the phrase "teachable moment" because it makes it sound like those moments pop up now and again. But the truth is that when you are with kids, every moment is teachable. They watch everything you do, they need guidance almost all the time, and every minute that they are awake and in your care, you are on duty.

I decided to rest my sciatica, so I finally picked up and read the first chapter of *The Feminine Mystique*. The book was published by W.W. Norton & Company in 1963, and the quotes in the first chapter are all from 1950s housewives. They say things like:

> My days are all busy, and dull, too. . . . I make breakfast, so I do the dishes, have lunch, do some more dishes and some laundry and cleaning in the afternoon. . . . The biggest time, I'm chasing kids.
>
> Very little of what I've done has been really necessary or important. Outside pressures lash me through the day. Yet I look upon myself as one of the more relaxed housewives in the neighborhood. Many of my friends

are even more frantic. . . . The American Housewife is once again trapped in a squirrel cage.

The book notes that women are going on tranquilizers and other medications in unprecedented numbers; women are complaining of depression or anxiety at a very high rate. It sounded a lot like today.

As I read quote after quote from these long-ago housewives, they could have been me, or any of my friends, speaking today. The things these women said were the exact same things we women complained about to each other at school drop-off or during soccer games. Had nothing changed? Did I go back to the 1950s to realize that nothing had changed?

the last days of
summer

Stop chafing-seam torture . . . no crotch seams . . . no seams anywhere!

—Silf Skin Pantie Girdle ad, 1955

Somebody knocked over all the bottles on my dressing table. And my pancake makeup is missing.

—June Cleaver,
Leave It to Beaver, "Black Eye," 1957

Mom, you are so beautiful. I mean it—you're like a movie star. Don't laugh; I'm not kidding. I'm serious—you're beautiful. You look just as good as all those people on TV.

—Sam, at a bedtime chat

Betty Friedan, the author of *The Feminine Mystique*, was a stay-at-home suburban mom with three kids, but she was actually writing secretly for women's magazines. She had been fired from a newspaper job when she was pregnant and admitted to feeling like a freak because she still wanted to work. But she kept it to herself, because working was not an acceptable thing for mothers to do.

The book talks about "the problem that has no name." They called it the problem that had no name because these women knew there was something wrong but they couldn't identify it. They had everything that was supposed to make them happy, and yet they weren't. The image of the happy housewife blissfully fulfilled by gleaming floors and tasty luncheon platters was something no woman could live up to. Or rather, when they did live up to it, they found it hollow. As more and more women married young, had kids, and stayed home to raise them, they felt dissatisfied. They loved their husbands and their kids. They were proud of their homes. Then why did they feel so empty or angry or desperate?

The "mystique" refers to the image of feminine fulfillment that was the gold standard for female living in the years after World War II. Millions of women aspired to nothing more than marriage, mother-hood, and a lovely home. This was their highest ambition, and they didn't think about the outside world and its problems.

This mystique was born organically, perhaps, because in the years after the war, home and hearth were uppermost in everyone's mind. But it was escalated by an advertising industry eager to sell women appliances, cleaning products, prepared foods, and furniture. Women were told what would make them happy, and many believed it. They wanted to believe it because it sounded so good.

The thinking of the day was that they couldn't be real women *and* work. That would destroy their sexuality. Besides, what job could be more fulfilling than that of housewife? Articles in women's maga-zines on famous actresses wouldn't speak of them enjoying their work or making money. Instead, they presented the actress in her home, cooking dinner or caring for her children, as if her career was just something to keep her busy while the kids were at school.

When the women availed themselves of the new household products, they did not use these advantages to free themselves or to lessen their load; they used the new products to create higher and more impossible standards of housekeeping. For instance, when they got the washer and dryer, instead of delighting in all the time they saved by not hanging clothes on the line and waiting for them to dry, a woman might simply start laundering more aggressively and changing the sheets twice a week.

The women were taught to put everyone else first and often ended up living vicariously through their children. Who can blame them? I'd be living through my kids too if I had to change the sheets twice a week.

My Kids Are Cute, and I Have the Scrapbook to Prove It

In between chapters of *The Feminine Mystique*, I finally decided to work on the photo albums. I spread out the pictures all over the dining room table. Sorting through them would have been overwhelming, except that it was summer, so I was able to devote an hour or two at a time to the job and then leave the photos spread out on the dining room table. We just ate dinner on the patio for the week.

I would hold up pictures and say, "Oh, Jack, look how cute you were!" "Sam, can you believe your hair then?" The kids were not interested. I had to force them to help me, and after about ten minutes of looking at pictures, Jack would say, "Can we turn on the TV now?"

Looking at the pictures, I was taken aback at how time had blurred. Only a few years had passed, but I could not distinguish Sam's third grade pictures from his fourth grade ones, and I couldn't remember which Halloween it was that Jack was a ninja; hence, it was really difficult to get the photos in chronological order. As I saw the images of the past three years spread before me, I became increasingly grateful for my slow summer. Half of me was completely sick of having the kids around me all the time, and the other half was deeply relieved to have the kids around me all the time. The pictures brought back all the Easter egg hunts, birthday parties, swim meets, Pinewood Derby races, and the trip to Hershey Park. There were pictures of my dad visiting us for Thanksgiving and then later at the beach house. He stood on the deck with a drink in his hand, laughing at some joke. There was a picture of Jack asleep on the floor in his coat. He used to come home from preschool so exhausted that he would sleep anywhere, and one time, I took a picture to prove it. Even the boring moments were bewitching because they were frozen in time. I looked up from these pictures and saw the boys. They didn't care about the pictures—they were more interested in TV. All the days in these pictures had been lived and were now mostly forgotten by our minds, which were too busy living to hold onto what was passing. I stared at the pictures. I was there for each one of these moments. It seemed impossible that I had lived that many moments.

Glue Sticks, Please

It was the last week of summer now, so we needed to buy school supplies. The list of things kids need for school these days would probably astonish most 1950s mothers. They include things like Purell, Post-its, and glue sticks, most of which weren't even around in the 50s.

Complete School Supply List (1950s)

- Pencils
- Cigar box
- Pencil sharpener
- Eraser

Partial School Supply List (Today)

- Antibacterial wipes
- Spiral notebooks
- Pocket folders
- Chisel-tip yellow highlighter
- Filler paper
- #2 Oriole sharpened latex-free pencils
- Large pink erasers, latex-free
- Washable glue sticks
- Marble notebooks
- Blue heavy-duty 3-round-ring binder
- Front-view cover spiral poly portfolio

I am not sure how a front-view cover spiral poly portfolio helps our children read or do long division. I do know this: at the end of every school year, I have stacks of partially filled marble notebooks left over that I don't throw out because it seems like a waste to toss a notebook that only has twelve pages used up. I save them for grocery lists and then forget to use them and then just end up throwing them out after all.

Most of my friends had already bought their supplies; many of them buy during July when the stores run their specials, but I never did that. I hated thinking about school in the middle of summer, even when I wasn't having a 1950s summer. Besides, I always thought it was fun to cram it in right before school started. I pictured us bustling off to the store with our lists, filling our shopping cart, paying with a sizable discount coupon, and then coming home and cheerfully assembling it all by putting glue sticks in boxes, sharpening pencils, and labeling folders. Then we would put it all in the boys' backpacks and zip it up, ready for the year.

We went to Office Depot with the aforementioned sizable coupon. As I squinted my way through the lists and tried to find everything, the kids just darted away from me. They saw acquaintances, spun around in the ergonomic chairs, and threw stuff in the cart. "I found erasers, Mom!" one would shout before he ricocheted off to the next aisle. I couldn't keep track of what we were buying. I couldn't find the pocket folders, and I wished I'd had a snack before this because I was starving and the checkout line was about twenty people long. As we stood waiting, Sam begged me to buy him some giant jar of candy, I refused, the boys bickered, we smoldered and crept along, and Jack cried when Sam hit him too hard. I was at my wit's end.

We got home, and I sent them to their rooms to read. Couldn't we do ANYTHING without it turning into a circus? Why did they have to fight so much? Needless to say, I didn't feel like cheerfully sharpening pencils and labeling folders. I shoved all the bags aside in a corner of the dining room.

I thought I would go crazy if we had to stay home one more day. It would have been great if some friends called us, but no one did. Many of our friends were out of town, but frankly, I always felt like I was the one who would call other moms to plan outings or make playdates. When I mentioned this to other mothers, they all said they felt the same way. You would think that all of us who were at home would have a busy schedule of park, pool, or little trips to keep the kids busy and ourselves happy. But instead, I often felt alone. I felt like the only one who wanted to go into the city or who needed to get out of the house. Other moms seemed to have extended families and cousins, errands to do, husbands who take off a day during the week, or any manner of little breaks to help them out.

This loneliness gets blamed on suburbia, but really, I think it's just motherhood.

Jackson Pollock and Fries

Thank goodness we did have a few outings in mind for the final week before Labor Day.

We had planned to go to the Metropolitan Museum of Art one day this summer because Sam had a museum treasure hunt that his upcoming sixth grade teacher had assigned. I tried to coordinate this with other mothers so that we could go in a group with friends from his class, but I couldn't find anybody else who wanted to go. (See above.)

The hunt was age appropriate and pretty fun. The kids were challenged to find eight specified items in the museum (a portrait of George Washington, a modern painting, etc.). If you did, you got to go to a special lunch with the teacher in the fall. Miracle of miracles, Sam *wanted* to do this.

I love the Met, and had been dragging my kids there since they were babies. Just walking into that place calms me down. Being surrounded by statues and artifacts that are hundreds of years old gives me the sense that I belong to a part of the time-space continuum. All those artists struggled to live and work, and they left something of value behind. Walking among those things reminds me that I am a part of something larger than my daily life.

I also took them there because I wanted them to like the things that I like. As it happens, they liked the things that *they* liked. They liked running through enclosed places, sitting down on every bench or chair they passed, touching anything off limits, and listening to their voices echo in places they shouldn't be shouting. They liked the gift shop. And they liked eating.

Inexplicably, during any kind of cultural outing, they were starving. At home, a baloney sandwich and a banana was a decent lunch. Once we got to an overpriced cafeteria, however, their appetites were bottomless. We needed pizza, burgers, cheese fries, an apple, water, chocolate milk, and maybe a smoothie. We needed dessert, but which one? The extra-large cupcakes? The pudding parfait? And also, Mom, can I have chips AND fries?

We found the paintings and other art on the homework list. I'm not sure how much sank in, though, because the boys spent most of their time poking, teasing, and hanging onto each other. No fewer than six different security guards had to tell us, "No touching!" The inside of the walk-through Egyptian tomb "smelled funny." Jack, his legs "about to fall off!" sprawled out on a bench and inadvertently kicked an elderly man. Upon seeing the Jackson Pollock paintings, both boys declared, "I could do that."

Finally, it was time for lunch—the boys' favorite part. They got very creative—for instance, they discovered how delicious it was to dip your French fry into the custard of your Boston cream donut. "I just made up a new dessert!" Jack exclaimed.

During these three and a half hectic hours of kid wrangling, an occasional moment of appreciation dawned. Jack noticed how beautiful the light in the sculpture garden was, and Sam recognized a figure he had read about in mythology. After lunch, we found a painting of a place we might want to live, a charming garden-and-grotto scene from about two hundred years ago. "That's really great," Sam said as he stared at it. Then he turned to me, reverie broken, and said, "Can we get a snack?"

We got home, exhausted. That is, I was exhausted. The boys had enough energy left to run all over the house and shout and fight.

The next day, we just stayed home and hit the pool. Since we did something the day before, we needed a no-plans day afterward. The boys couldn't handle too much enlightenment.

So I worked on the photo albums and resisted the temptation to make a career to-do list for next week. One of my friends called; she got a teaching job. We had walked home from many a school day together, the kids running all around us, and she had worked long and hard to get her master's. It was finally her turn. She was so excited. Her kids were older than mine, and she was more than ready to get out of the house. As she put it, "The kids don't need me. They just want me there so I can put their Pop-Tart in for them. If I hang around the house, I just end up being everybody's slave."

I know the feeling.

The Feminine Mystique Fifty Years Later

I was still reading *The Feminine Mystique.*

One of the more striking observations in Friedan's book was this: the most important function a woman served in that society was to buy more things for the house.

Of course! It all made so much sense. The advertisers created an image for you to live up to, and to do so, you needed an army of products. Products that made your life easier, your figure prettier, your children healthier, and your husband happier.

The thing is, the more you bought into this belief system, the easier it was to be distracted from real life (Terrible Trivium!). The housewife believed that she had to keep things spotless and charming. She could easily fill her days with repetitive tasks that would eat away her time. This conveniently kept her from making any real choice concerning who she was and what she wanted.

Women still buy most of the stuff for the household. We buy the food, the clothes, the cleaning products, and the décor for the house. And now, in case you haven't noticed, houses are bigger than ever. Our culture promotes huge master bedrooms with walk-in closets, great rooms, home theaters in the basement, and outdoor kitchens. This last one I find particularly galling. I thought the whole women's movement was to help get us OUT of the kitchen, and now the darn thing has *followed us outside*! More appliances to scrub clean, more ways to cook, more places to serve and eat. Help me.

All these rooms need more furniture, more TVs, more stuff to hang on the wall. Kitchens now need huge islands, some of them bigger than my dining room table. We think our big kitchens will bring our families together. We believe in big, roomy SUVs. We think those cars will allow us to go exciting places. We believe in laptops, cell phones, and websites. We think those things will keep us connected.

And yet we're no more connected than we were fifty years ago. A kitchen is a kitchen; a car is a car. We run and run to get more, have more, and do more. We've been empowered to have careers and make money, but have those paychecks made us feel more secure and comfortable? Or have we simply used that money to create higher and more impossible standards of living?

We are told by the advertising industry that a consumer lifestyle will make us happy. We believe it, and we chase that dollar.

I Can't Help It; I Love Waterslides

One of the things I had been waiting to do all summer was visit Tomahawk Lake, an old-fashioned water park about an hour away. It is built alongside a lake in a rustic setting with musty (mostly clean) bathrooms and tons of picnic tables and charcoal grills. There are sections on the beach for toddlers with little water play areas, sections for older kids, and sections for picnicking. Around the curve of the lake are several different waterslides, all of which deposit you into the lake. It is very spread out, so even on crowded days, the place is still shady and peaceful. There is a snack stand where you can buy burgers and fries, a soft-serve ice cream stand, and a miniature golf course. The kids love it there, but probably nobody loves it more than I do. I never get tired of waterslides. I drag my inflatable tube up the hill while the lifeguards try to be polite about the damp, middle-aged woman who flies down the same rides over and over again.

Bill was iffy about going; the weather was cloudy and cool. The kids were on the fence, too. They liked Tomahawk Lake, but to be honest, they would have been just as happy if we let them stay home and play video games all day. So we had a family conference in the living room to debate the issue. We tried to figure out what we would do if we DIDN'T go to the water park, and the kids said no to everything we suggested, probably because they were just waiting for us to suggest they play video games all day. Eventually, the conversation got so repetitive and unproductive that Bill laid down on the floor, bored. So the boys climbed on Bill, which led to wrestling, which led to laughing and even some screaming. We still couldn't decide what to do. We had the giggles.

During a lull in the laughter, Sam asked, "Why can't we just do this all day?"

Why not, indeed?

Eventually, the laughing died down, someone got kicked, and things were about to morph into yelling. We did go to Tomahawk Lake after all, and it was perfect. It was not crowded, the weather held, and we went on the slides over and over again because there were no lines. We ate the lunch I packed, and then we got soft-serve ice cream. We rode the slides as a family, laughing and shouting to each other. We were all enjoying the same thing at the same time—a miracle.

Summer's Last Perfect Day

The next day was the Sunday of Labor Day weekend. We were guests at a lake club with a large group of friends. These were Bill's friends from college; most of them were married with kids. The club was a place just out of the 1950s (What is it with lakes? Are they all frozen in time?). There were little grills, and picnic tables were scattered around the edge of the lake; there were rowboat races and Ping-Pong tables in screened huts. There were bear warning horns on the trees, although it was unclear what you were supposed to do if you heard the siren. We had all brought food to cook and share, and the kids ranged in age from about five years old to college age. Old friends, young kids, and a beautiful setting gave the day a timeless feeling. The hours passed slowly and beautifully.

Around dusk, a bunch of us went out in rowboats. Sam and I took one out together. He insisted on rowing, which he had never done before. He picked it up easily and proudly rowed me way out into the lake. The trees against the setting sun were beautiful. Sam told me how much he loved this, and I teasingly called him nature boy. He stopped rowing and we drifted. I looked at him—the setting sunlight glowing

on his skin, his gaze settling on the trees far away, his gangly legs trying to arrange themselves in the shallow boat. It was a moment free of
forward motion.

Over the summer, while he was doing nothing, he grew up a little.
He was a boy who could get into a rowboat and row it well on the first
try. He was a boy who could notice beauty. He was a boy who could say,
"Mom, let me row. You relax. I'll do it."

back to the routine

I'm FREE as a bird! with my Westinghouse 100% Automatic Defrosting refrigerator.

—Westinghouse ad, 1952

I can't have any coffee . . . I've got to get home and scrub that darn kitchen floor.

—Myrtle, the neighbor,
Father Knows Best, "Margaret's Premonition," 1955

You snored last night.

—Bill, to me, on many a morning

L abor Day. Summer was officially over. I woke up bone tired. I thought I was getting a sore throat. The house was filthy. (How could that be when all I did the past month was clean!?) In any case, it was the last day that the pool was open, so I figured I'd worry about the mess tomorrow.

The pool was crowded. Like us, many families were enjoying one last time in the water. Dads (including Bill) were in the shallow end with their kids climbing all over them. I jumped off the diving board over and over again. Flying through the air and plunging deeply through the bright blue water seemed like the best way to say good-bye to the place where I had spent so many happy and relaxing afternoons. The lifeguards gave out free ice cream on the last day. I ate two pops in a greedy attempt to cram in as much summer as possible. I couldn't believe the season was over. How could a slow summer go so fast?

When the pool closed, we dragged our feet as we left. My stomach actually tightened as I walked out the gate to the car, knowing I would have to wait two hundred plus days before I returned to the delightful ruckus of wet, shouting kids, shaded picnic tables, and lazy conversations on lawn chairs. At home, we had burgers on the grill. The boys skipped their bath for the fourth day in a row.

School started Wednesday, so I had Tuesday to get organized. I was up early doing laundry, cleaning, and trying to get the boys to help. I sent them out to clean the car, and Jack wrote "kick me" all over Sam with a marker he found in the backseat. They were laughing, and it was kind of funny, but I wouldn't miss it tomorrow.

I felt the tension already. I had not expected this day to be stressful. I had thought I would enjoy the actions of getting back in the swing, that the kids would be tired and compliant, and that I would have a productive, bustling day and feel good about the end of my 1950s summer.

Instead, I was a total crab. The kids were wildly noncompliant, as they had been all summer, except that during the summer, not much was required of them, so it didn't matter. But now it DID matter; there were pencils to be sharpened and Legos to be picked up. We had spent the past months just playing with blocks and Legos for hours on end then kind of just sliding it off to the side of the living room, going to the pool, going to bed, and sliding the blocks and Legos out again the next day. That was over. We would be way too busy to enjoy such extended Lego involvement during the week, and we needed to put it away.

I couldn't even get sentimental about them going back to school. I just kept thinking of all that was still undone. I was fully back to the present day—to the pressure and the unending lists. That night, Bill couldn't sleep. He thought it was because he was stressed about summer ending and fall pressures starting. Fall used to be a season of fun and promise, and now it just felt crushing.

Start Your Engines!

On the first day of school, we were all up early, of course, and ready to go. Sam was very eager. He was always ready to go back to school in the fall. Jack was ready, but I wouldn't call him eager.

We walked to school; it was only two blocks away. Sam, a bit startled, asked, "Dad is coming too?" I could tell he was embarrassed, so I told Sam to walk ahead. He did. But when we got there, many Dads were there, and we all took pictures, chatted, laughed. I felt a stab when I saw other moms with a baby on their hip, or a darling toddler in a stroller, and I wished I had another baby.

Then again, I was not even going to the bagel breakfast after drop-off. The PTO always sponsored a bagel breakfast in the gym. Parents could go pick up flyers with PTO information and have coffee. Younger siblings of students were welcome, so there were tons of preschoolers and toddlers running around. It was always a great way to connect with moms you hadn't seen all summer, and the little kids loved it. I used to go to this every year and looked forward to it. But that year, for the first time, I had no interest. I already was as involved with the PTO as I wanted to be. I didn't have a toddler I needed to keep busy for the morning, and I had my whole week planned to be just for me. It was only a three-day week, and I was getting back to work. I had a column due, and I was squeezing in the gym, a haircut, a pedicure, extra house cleaning, and some long dog walks.

I lingered in the crowd on the blacktop. Parents everywhere hugged their kids one last time, snapped a picture, and waved as the children filed into the building. The second bell rang. The blacktop emptied. Summer was gone, and here I was again, same place, same pace, same frenzy.

We walked home, and Bill left for work right away. Then the phone rang, and my friend Stacey and I had a good, long chat. After I hung up, the house was quiet. I missed the boys. What were they doing now? I missed them emptying the blocks out on the floor with a clatter and hopping around in their PJs digging up Legos and creating new things. I had work to do, tons of it, so I didn't need to stand there—still— thinking about them. But I did.

From Zero to Sixty in One Short Week

I really had missed working, and it felt wonderful to again have dead-lines and conference calls and feel the rhythm. But it felt terrible to be pulled in a million directions. In a single hour, I threw in some laundry, did research on a column, emailed some contacts, filled out a vaccina-tion form for Sam, read through my class mom obligations, took some meat out of the freezer, wrote the opening paragraph on my next piece, and stepped over stacks of paperwork I knew I wouldn't get to for at least two weeks. Everywhere I turned in the house, there was a chore waiting to be done.

Sam tried out for, and got chosen to do, the morning announce-ments at school for the month of September. He started soccer, Boy Scouts picked up again, band rehearsals began. Jack brought home so much homework in the first two weeks he actually cried. I had forgot-ten how frustrating it was to have a list that never got completed. How was it that the schedule had already completely taken over our lives?

The weather was still hot and sunny, and the boys' feet were filthy at night because they ran around in bare feet after school. It made me miss summer even more: we were on a fall schedule, but the weather was calling us to come outside and play.

Sam walked to school by himself early now for the announcements. At first he didn't want to . . . he wasn't used to doing things by himself. I tried to assure him it was OK; there is a crossing guard at one of the streets. I had walked him part of the way a few times, and then one morning, he was ready to do it himself. He hugged me tightly, a big hug, kissed my cheek, and headed down the driveway. I watched his head bobbing down the sidewalk, then he broke into a jog around the corner and disappeared out of view. And just like that, another milestone was reached.

Of course I was happy for him, and for me. Any time your child takes a healthy step toward adulthood is cause for pride and relief. But I'd be lying if I didn't say a little part of me died inside. There are so many places he is going to go without me.

That was the beginning of his sixth grade year. I knew he would begin to change. He would get pimples and eventually "man" hair on his legs. I'd seen it happen to other boys. I felt so profoundly grateful for my slow summer. Over those months, I had little kids. Kids who brought home fistfuls of dusty rocks and left them on the kitchen counter. Kids who teased each other to the point of tears but then fell asleep in the same bed, entwined and sweaty. Kids who could really stress you out—or give you a perfect summer.

What I Learned on My Summer Vacation

I was behind on housework and my writing already. I read all those Household Hints, but I was still a sloppy housewife. I never taught the kids how to do laundry or unload the dishwasher during the summer.

I certainly didn't figure out how to manage our time better, because we were already drowning in the list of things to do.

The kids had a great summer. They were totally free. Free to be bored, to daydream, to bicker, and to ramble and run through their days as they chose. I was freer, too. I watched them more closely, I enjoyed them daily—maybe not every second of the day, but there was definitely enjoyment. My goal was just to slow down enough so that I could really pay attention. I did that, and I liked what I saw.

As we stand on the other side of the 1950s, we all understand that many women want the fulfillment that comes from having a career. Most of us are not wealthy, so we work to pay the bills and buy those family necessities. We crave challenging, interesting work to be happy, well-rounded people. But it isn't true that simply having a career is the secret to a woman's happiness, because if it were, we'd all be little balls of bliss floating through our days. Instead, we are just as anxious and frustrated as our forerunners were. We may do it all, but we don't do it all well, so we have a nagging sense of failure. It's supposed to be easier than this, right?

What About Love?

In the 1950s, you could blame women's lack of fulfillment on the fact that they left college or skipped college to get married, stayed home with their children, and perhaps never got the chance to challenge themselves. But most women today work after high school and college. We don't expect motherhood and marriage to be our sole fulfillment. So why, when we "have everything," does it still feel like something is missing?

You can try to find the answer by analyzing data, quoting studies, dissecting economic trends, etc. But all that clinical observation leaves one thing out. It leaves out love. No amount of education or financial success can compete with the love that comes when you have a family. You have the college degree, you have years of experience, you love your job, and you have a supportive husband. You know you can handle it all, and you plan it out carefully. Then you have a little boy with drool on his chin and light in his eyes, and your plans change.

Maybe you quit work; maybe you go down to part time. Maybe you keep the same hours and still thrive in your career. But you're not the same person. That love has changed you, and now, parceling up your days into separate hours of work, marriage, cleaning, and child care is not as easy as you thought it would be.

This love is what pulls us apart. There is no easy decision when dividing up your hours between your children, your husband, and your job. We have seen a trend of highly educated, affluent women giving up their jobs to stay home with their children. I don't think these women are rejecting feminism or hiding from adult responsibilities. I think they're just tired of dividing themselves up into so many little pieces. So, if they have the financial freedom to quit work, they do.

What Am I Trying to Live Up To?

It's easy to intellectualize it all and quote statistics about how much housework husbands do or how the glass ceiling is not disappearing. But that only tells part of the story. It doesn't tell about how every now and then, you get a sense of how quickly time is passing, and you feel that desperate ache to stop it and keep your kids at the age where they will crawl into your lap and snuggle. You can't stop time, and you know this, but you can stop what you're doing that moment and make your lap available. You can spend a half an hour, or an hour, or an afternoon with them. It's not about the cutest thing they say or the milestone they reach that day. It's about how you're just together, and that's all.

It can be lonely and frustrating to be at home all day or to cut back on your own goals to be with your children, but everything has a cost, and the more valuable things are, the more they cost. Spending time with your children costs a tremendous amount.

Several months before my 1950s summer, I had been working with a collaborator on a musical. As we finished up our writing session one evening, I said to her, "I should be home by eight thirty. The kids should be finished with their homework, and hopefully they've had their bath and are in bed." She, a mother of two herself, chuckled and suggested I lower my expectations.

I laughed, and I saw that she was right. And then I saw that she was right in a far deeper way than simply hoping the kids were already in bed. Most of the frustration I feel is from trying to live up to something that can't be. We should just lower our expectations. We should simply expect our kids to be noisy, disruptive, silly, and sloppy. We should expect our house to be a money pit. We should expect that our careers will be a slog of difficult days, hard work, and boredom, with a few exciting successes thrown in.

Just like our 1950s forerunners, we believe what we see on TV. We believe the magazines and websites. We don't just read those stories and see those pictures as fun ideas or escape; we see them as what we're all supposed to have. We're supposed to have fancy kitchens, Jacuzzi bathtubs, warm family game nights around the Wii, a new SUV every few years, and exciting vacations to Disney or Atlantis. Your children didn't swim with the dolphins? What kind of mother are you?

Every generation asks the question "Is this all there is?" We started out young, knowing what we wanted, and then when we got it, it didn't seem enough. Or it seemed like too much. In any case, it was not quite right. How do we stop the relentless forward motion—the motion that blurs the rich life on either side of us?

A Dose of Perspective

A couple of weeks later, I finally finished the photo albums. I had two tidy books of perfectly arranged photographs. The dining room table was cleared off and able to be dined upon again. I had a huge sense of satisfaction. There is something about a book of chronologically arranged photographs that allows you to feel like you're really on top of things, even if it isn't true. Bill and I looked at them together; I could tell he really appreciated the work they took.

Other than that accomplishment, I was discouraged. None of my writing projects were going anywhere. Did I make a mistake in taking time off? I was exhausted all the time, tense, and overwhelmed.

I finished a column earlier than expected and turned on the TV for some mindless chatter to cheer me up. The kids had been watching their own channels during breakfast earlier, so the *Jimmy Neutron* theme song came on. I instantly had a stab of missing the kids. I missed them laying around in their PJs watching morning TV. I missed their presence. And I missed being with them in the absence of pressure. My time with them since school started was spent shepherding them through tasks: homework, music practice, chores. There was so little time to simply enjoy each other.

I switched the channel to find a pleasant morning talk show, and the September 11 remembrance ceremonies were on. I had forgotten what day it was.

I can remember very clearly what 9/11 was like in this house. Living in the New York City area that day meant that your family member, friend, or neighbor might not be coming home again. Like all Americans, we experienced the shock and horror of an attack on our country, but for those of us who lived here, it was also an attack on the places where we lived and worked. When we saw the footage of people running through the streets, we saw office buildings where we had jobs, delis where we bought coffee, subway stops we used regularly. We all knew people who worked downtown. What was happening to them?

Bill was safe. He had been on his way into the city when the planes hit, so he simply turned around and came home before he was even at the George Washington Bridge.

Sam was four, starting his second year of preschool. We let him stay upstairs and watch Nickelodeon on our bed for five hours. Jack was too young to understand, so he just played with toys on the floor while we watched the news coverage on TV.

Later that day, I took the kids to the park. The weather was gorgeous. The kids played, and parents talked on their cell phones, checking on friends and relatives. We adults spoke in code to each other: "Everybody OK?" Meaning, *Is your family alright?* Usually, they were.

The Simple Joys of Childhood

A few days after 9/11, that Saturday, I took the kids to a program at the library. They had a clown. There were tons of babies and toddlers and parents, and we were all there to see a clown. She was a sweet and funny clown, not a scary one. The kids loved her, and they laughed and each got a balloon animal. We adults were happy. It was the first time in several days it felt OK to be happy. Our children laughing and seeing something new was exactly what we all needed. We had permission to laugh, since we were laughing along with our children. It was a relief to feel optimistic. The power of children's joy in just being and growing was unmistakably healing.

That's what I wanted from my summer: to have the time to revel in the joy of children growing up. Growing up in their own happy way: a ramshackle, unforced way. With their noise and their mess and their free-form discoveries reminding me that you don't have to play by the rules. You don't have to have a schedule or goals. You can make things up as you go along.

As Jack says when complaining about one of his friends, "He talks too much. He spends too much time making up the rules, and there's no time left to play."

We took our time to play. We didn't follow the rules of the present; indeed, the best thing about thinking about the 1950s was that it freed me from the present day and all the rules we follow now. With that perspective, I saw quite clearly how speed had taken over all of our lives and that way too often, all I did was obey the pace of life without regard to why.

Pace and pressure are seductive temptresses, promising enticing rewards if you simply keep up. As the years have passed, it's been a struggle to keep in mind the lessons of slowing down and resist the urge to conform. One look at Facebook can send me careening back into the land of "Everyone is doing so much better than I am; I better get going!"

But I have seen that it will never slow down. If you want to take time, you have to take it. Literally take it. Take it away from something else. Take it, grab it, be in charge of it. I am always trying to get back to the slow place I created that summer. I take any opportunity: snow days, vacation days, summer—any time I can to jump off the merry-go-round. When I can't stop the motion, I sometimes just turn down the radio in the car and try to have some kind of meaningful talk with the kids as we drive to wherever we're going.

No Need to Rush

What I realized, and continue to realize through the years, is that I cannot simultaneously spend the right amount of time with the people I love AND have a perfect house or big career. Other women can—I've seen them do it, and I sometimes feel guilty and embarrassed that I can't. I am too tired or too distracted or too anxious or too *something*. Being with my children, cooking dinner for neighbors, and listening to my friends takes time. A lot of time. An absurd amount of time.

As busy as I was when the kids were in grade school, it got even worse as they got older. High school presented another minefield for those of us trying to walk our own road. It becomes ridiculously easy to worry about "falling behind." Everybody else's kids take AP classes, go to Europe on the exchange program, do well on the SATs, get a car when they get their license, have clear skin, get a summer job, and love to read books. Life becomes a series of checklists, and if you can't check off the right boxes (enriching summer camp: check! attractive prom date: check!), then you have failed your child. Who knows how they will end up?

What does that mean—*end up*? Is the end when your child goes to college? What they do after college? How much money will they make? What happens if they backpack through China or start their own business or wind up living in your basement? At what point are they "finished"?

I think about my father, who cruelly lost so many of his favorite things. His retirement years should have been a fulfillment of all his work and savings so that he could savor whatever pleased him. But that was not to be. Really, there is no use rushing to the end, because the end is no guarantee of anything. The moments I spent with my children that summer—the quiet moments of Legos in the morning or dinners on the patio, or the crazy ones where we screamed down waterslides or jumped off the diving boards—they are small pieces of fulfillment. They stick in my head and my heart like snapshots, moments caught in time already receding into the past.

I took the boys for haircuts. It was their "back to school" haircut, but school had already been in session for three weeks. We sandwiched it in between delivering mums for the Boy Scout fundraiser, soccer games, cleaning out our dresser drawers, shopping for christening presents for two different babies, and church. "Hectic" was the name of the game.

I watched their summery bleached-blond locks get snipped and fall to the floor. The kids, oblivious, played video games in their salon chairs. When finished, they looked neat and handsome. While they ran out to the front for their post-haircut lollipop, their summer hair was swept up by a broom and put in the trash.

And all I could think was: *I can't wait for next June.*

a handy reference guide to that simpler time

When did raising children get so complicated? I'm pretty sure it started around the 1980s, when "important research" started showing that fetuses could get smarter if you played Mozart on your abdomen. Insecure, upwardly-mobile parents strapped headphones to their baby bumps and then proceeded to glom on to every other trend that promised to protect, improve, and ascend their children.

Soon, an industry of child-centered products flourished, fed by parents who seemed to have more money but less confidence than parents of yore. Things eventually frothed to a ridiculous level as parents routinely peeled off hundreds of dollars for a fancy humidifier, a *French for Toddlers* DVD, or tennis lessons for their three-year-old. (That would be me.)

Concurrent with this obsession, women entered the workforce in larger and larger numbers and began using daycare, nannies, etc., to keep their children occupied. Once you start paying for it, you want it to be better. So if I am just at home with my kids, watching TV and doing a puzzle are fine, but if I am paying two thousand dollars a month, darn it, I want my four-year-old reading and learning math skills.

Children became investments. They had always been seen as a reflection of their parents, but now more than ever, we parents feel judged by the success—or lack of it—that our children display.

Good-bye, childhood. Hello, apprenticeship.

In jumped the ad industry. Capitalizing on the rise of these child-centered families, it began marketing specifically to children. Aspirational marketing, which appeals to children's "older" selves, offered them young versions of adult products like music (Kidz Bop) or fashion (Uggs come in baby sizes) or electronics (LeapPad) that made the child feel like a grown-up. Cannily designed to entice and manipulate, these ads worked hard to make sure kids grew up faster and started spending sooner. Once little kids could act like grown-ups, the window of time in which children actually wanted to be children shrank. And the more the kids acted like grown-ups, the more tempting it was to treat them like one, and suddenly you're looking at your eight-year-old thinking: *Shouldn't he be doing something more productive than pretending to be Spiderman?* (Yes, that's me again.)

I was in grade school in the 1960s and 1970s. I was not expected to be productive. I roamed our suburban neighborhood freely. My friends and I rode bikes in the street, ran through people's backyards, and did a lot of stuff that my parents never knew about. Not that it was a secret, but there was no need to talk about the fact that Debbie Catelli wore a bra instead of an undershirt or Betty O'Neal's bunny got out again and we spent the whole afternoon chasing it. Our parents didn't control our days. If I didn't like what game my friends were playing, I would go home and lie on my bed and read. There was nothing to watch on TV. There was no schedule. I didn't have to worry what time it was because I never had to be anywhere except for school and dinner. Apart from school and a few chores, my days were truly free, and I spent them doing whatever I liked.

My children were clearly craving the freedom that I had grown up with, and I wanted to give it to them. But how?

Forty years ago, parents were not expected to design each and every day as a cavalcade of delight for their children, but in my life, I was expected to do so. Given any free time, my kids became picky little tyrants. "Want to have David over?" I'd ask.

"He's boring!"

"Want to go to the museum and see the dinosaurs?"

"That's boring!"

"Hey, since it's a half day, how about we play mini golf and then get Burger King?"

"We did that last time!"

The pressure of the empty day was relentless.

Here's the number-one lesson from the "old days": children were expected to entertain themselves. It was NOT Mom's job to occupy or improve them. The children decided for themselves how they spent their play time, and whatever they came up with, as long as it was mostly safe, was acceptable. Parents did not assess their games and decide if that play was an appropriate use of the kid's time. If the kid just dug in the dirt or rode bikes around the block all day, that was fine. It was not looked upon as some colossal waste of a day that could have been better off spent at baseball camp.

Can we let our kids be that free now? Can you just send them off to the park? Well, not really. If you sent a couple of ten-year-olds off to the park to play, there is a good chance there will be no other kids their age at the park to play with. There would be toddlers with mothers or nannies; little preschool children would be running all over, having a wonderful time. Our society believes that outdoor free play and exercise is very important for the preschool set. But for school-age children, ages six to eleven, free play has all but disappeared. Our society thinks that kids that age have outgrown the need and desire for that type of play, so we keep kids in that age group busy after school. Whether rural, urban, or suburban, America's kids are all too booked to play. They are engulfed in the "getting ahead" activity list, and older kids, say eight or ten, are truly considered too old to be playing after school. They have homework and music lessons and sports practice. They have work to do.

Every society reproduces itself, so we are raising our kids to function in the world as it is now: hectic and structured with long days of work and lots of technology. We are not going to be able to give our kids that old-fashioned freedom all the time, and we should NOT feel guilty about it. It's not our fault there has been a seismic shift in the culture and economics of family life. Nonetheless, there are ways to make our days less stressful and give kids some independent play if we want to. There are three simple things you need to do. (I said they're simple. They are not easy.)

1. Find a safe place for the kids to play with no or minimal supervision from you.

2. Create a vacuum—a few hours where there is nothing for them to do *and they are totally unplugged.*

3. Get other kids together—get two, three, or twenty-five kids, also unplugged, together.

The place: It could be your backyard, or it could be a park. If it is a public park, you may need to go along with them and keep an eye out. This is fine, but sit on the bench and read or talk to a friend. Do not involve yourself in their games.

The time: During this time, they must be unplugged from all phones and video games. This will force them to play other things. Get ready for whining.

The kids: This chunk of time is free for them to do what they want. There is an excellent chance they will do stuff you don't approve of: fight, play rough, get filthy playing in wet mud, or just sit there pouting. Pretend not to notice.

Here are some suggestions of games from the '50s, '60s, and '70s. They usually revolved around being outside and using your imagination.

Games for the backyard/park/playground:

- **Store** : Set up boxes with play food or old cans; grab some bags and maybe that old Fisher Price register or a calculator to tally items. They can even set up some type of board on a slant so they can roll the items down to simulate the conveyer belt. Let the kids shop away.

- **War:** Two opposing sides battle. They can use play swords, play guns, or water guns or pretend they are shooting arrows, etc. They can even just tag to capture each other.

- **Castle:** Like war, except you have a castle to attack/defend. The "castle" can be your garage, or a jungle gym, or just a group of trees.

- **Dress Up:** Keep a box of old clothes/hats/Halloween costumes. They can dress up as a specific thing—superhero, astronaut, doctor, etc.—or just make it up with funny combinations. Once they are dressed, they will usually play pretend as that character.

- **Tea Party:** Not just for girls! We had a plastic tea set, and the boys would set it up with their action figures, and then the "guests" would purposely have bad manners and spill the pretend tea . . . Spiderman chewed with his mouth open . . . you get the idea.

- **House (with variations: Prairie House, Beach House, etc.):** This can be set up anywhere inside or outside. Kids play the dad, mom, baby, grandma, dog, neighbor, whoever or whatever.

- **Hide and Seek:** Outside or inside, it never gets old.

- **Band:** Use play instruments or pots and wooden spoons, and they could be a marching band. They can even mime having a trumpet and make the sounds themselves.

- **School:** Set up chairs and a "blackboard." Kids take turns being the teacher and calling on students, etc.

- **Follow the Leader:** Kids line up and the leader walks around marching, singing, jumping over a log, etc. Kids follow the leader's actions.
- **Simon Says:** The leader, "Simon," gives a direction to the other players, using the name first (i.e., "Simon says, 'Touch your toes'" or "Simon says, 'Whistle.'") Players obey directions. Simon will occasionally give a direction without first specifying "Simon says." Anyone following a direction that is not prefaced by "Simon says" is out.
- **Charades:** You may have to play this with them a few times until they get the hang of it.
- **Good Guys vs. Bad Guys:** (This could be cops/robbers, superheroes/villains, Jedi/aliens, etc.) The same concept as War, but may include a jail for the bad guys or other place to capture the enemy.
- **Tag (or Freeze Tag):** There are so many fun variations on this—Toilet Tag (they flush your extended arm to unfreeze you), Monster Tag (freeze in the pose of your favorite monster), Candle Tag (when tagged, you melt—someone needs to untag you before you melt to the ground), Amoeba Tag (you tag and join hands, growing bigger and bigger, and then split when you have four), etc.
- **Leapfrog:** Best for the younger set because there is no clear "win" here. Kids take turns crouching down while another child "leaps" over their back by placing their hands on the crouched person's back and vaulting over them. Leaping continues in a line or circle with the last person leaping to the front and then starting again.
- **Hopscotch:** No need to go to a playground—you can draw your own on a sidewalk or driveway.
- **Box Ball (also called Foursquare):** You need a ball (like a kickball) and a large, paved area for this. Some schools or playgrounds have this painted on the ground, or you can bring your own chalk and draw a large square divided into four

equal quadrants, each one about four by four feet, numbered one to four. The Number One player serves, bouncing the ball to any player. The player must return the ball to any other square with just one bounce and using only one touch to the ball. The ball is bounced from one square to the others. If it bounces out of a player's box, that player is out and everyone moves up a square. Players try to get to Number One.

- **Duck, Duck, Goose:** Children sit in a circle; one player is "it" and stands up behind them. He taps each person on the head as he walks around the circle. With each tap, he declares, "Duck, duck, duck." When he taps someone and calls them "goose," the goose must get up and chase the tapper around the circle. If the goose can't catch him before he makes his way all around the circle and sits down in the goose's spot, then the goose becomes "it."

- **Kick the Can:** A can (bucket, paint can, etc.) is placed in the middle of a field or yard. One person is "it"—they cover their eyes while all other players hide. Then the "it" person tries to find and tag the other players. When she does, that player goes to jail. Any free player can kick the can (tip it over) to free a jailed person. Players are freed in the order in which they were captured. The game continues until all players are captured or the person caught tipping the can is tagged.

- **Red Rover:** Kids make two lines opposite each other across a field. They link hands to make a chain. One line shouts to the other, naming a kid to send over. ("Red rover, red rover, send Mikey right over!") The kid tries to barrel through the chain, breaking through clasped hands. If the child succeeds, the two whose hands broke return to the opposing team. If he does not succeed, he must join that team, and the madness continues.

- **Red Light, Green Light:** One kid stands across the yard or park with her back to the rest of the kids. Back turned, she yells "Green light" and the kids start running toward her. At any point, she can yell "Red light" and turn around. When she turns around, all kids must be stopped, frozen in their tracks. Any kid still moving when she turns around is out. She returns to facing away from the kids and yells "Green light." This keeps going until someone reaches her and tags her before she can stop them with a "Red light."

- **Mother, May I?:** One child is the "mother," and all the other children line up facing her some distance away. The mother calls on each kid and tells them to "take one giant step" or "take three baby steps" toward her. The child must ask "Mother, may I?" before they move, and the mother will answer "yes" or "no." If they don't ask, they have to go back to the starting line. The first one to get up to "Mother" wins. You can use all kinds of steps: baby, giant, turning, crab steps, bunny hops, tiptoe, leap, etc.

- **Man in the Middle:** You need at least three people. Two people try to keep a ball or Frisbee away from the "man in the middle." When the middle guy catches the ball, the one who threw it has to rotate into the middle.

- **Capture the Flag:** Two teams each hide a piece of cloth—their flag. Then they try to find the other team's flag and capture it, taking it to their home base, all while avoiding being tagged by opposing team members.

- **Running Bases:** Set up two bases a good distance apart. The bases could be trees, a rock, a bush, a cone—anything. Two players throw a ball back and forth while other players try to run back and forth between the two bases without getting tagged by one of the throwers with the ball. If a runner gets tagged three times, he becomes a thrower.

- **Manhunt:** One person hides. Everyone looks for them. Great for large places—like three or four adjacent backyards. There are many variations on this, which you can find by searching it on the web, and it's great at night with flashlights.

- **Wall Ball:** You need a wall (like the side of a big building) and a small rubber ball or a tennis ball. Two or more people take turns throwing the ball at the wall, and another player catches it and throws it at the wall. There are many versions of this game with various rules; you can make it as competitive (missing the ball gets you out) or relaxed as the kids want it to be.

I can give these suggestions—and there are many others—but the truth is, they will be mostly unnecessary. Your children CAN play on their own; they do it at recess every day! Recess is the closest thing to old-fashioned free play that exists these days. During recess, kids may play pretend; they may play tag or kickball; they may just trace the sand with the tip of their shoe. They may not even be having fun; they may be miserably counting the minutes until the bell rings. The point is, they are free. No one is telling them what to play or how to play it or even to play at all. They decide for themselves.

Besides games, children could also:

- Go "camping" in the backyard: no official tent necessary; set up sheets and blankets and just sleep under the stars or zonk out on the trampoline.
- Build a fort: inside with pillows, or outside with whatever is around.
- Jump rope: you can get a long rope that two people operate and have the third person jump in; you can also get two ropes and have them going at once in "double Dutch" fashion.
- Put on a show: they can make one up or act out stuff they see on TV or in the movies, like scenes from *Toy Story* or *The Little Mermaid*, etc.
- Put on a puppet show: they can make puppets with old socks or just use their stuffed animals.
- Play with pots and pans and wooden spoons.
- Make mud pies: OK, I admit I've never done this. But I did let my kids play in huge mud puddles after rainstorms, kicking and splashing and getting soaked and filthy. Then they took a

long bath (with toys) while I did the laundry and had a cup of tea. Not a bad afternoon.

- Play with/in a big box: Use one from a delivery of an appliance or large item; the box can be a car, a spaceship, etc. Let kids draw, cut, or roll it.
- Plant seeds in the yard.
- Draw with chalk on the sidewalk/driveway.
- Fish in a stream.
- Feed ducks.
- Feed birds.

They might go through twenty ideas and then start complaining. Fine. Complaining is not going to kill them. Try filling a jar with ideas you and your kids come up with—they can read through them when they need some help in deciding what to do.

For those times when they can't play outside, they can have "unsupervised" play inside, too. Playing games with no adults involved lets the kids have all kinds of arguments: "We're going clockwise!" "No, we're going in order of age!" "He's cheating!" All that negotiating helps kids develop social skills and maturity. They can play some games that I've already listed, like House or Dress Up, or they can enjoy a board game.

Classic board games:

- **Cards:** Go Fish, Old Maid, Poker, Gin Rummy, Concentration, Solitaire
- Checkers
- Chess
- Life
- Monopoly
- Yahtzee
- Battleship
- Twister

- Operation
- Trouble
- Hands Down

If a child prefers to play by themselves instead of being with others, they might take up a hobby or some other solitary activity. Quiet hobbies allow kids some independence and the privacy of their own thoughts.

Activities and hobbies:

- Blowing bubbles
- Yo-yo
- Drawing/coloring
- Blocks, Legos, train tracks
- Dominoes
- Sewing
- Crocheting/knitting
- Baking
- Building model airplanes/rockets
- Caring for an easy pet (fish, hamster, lizard)
- Collecting (shells, rocks, stamps, coins, etc.)
- Inventing a new game
- Daydreaming

The children should be doing something on their own. They get freedom—and you get time for yourself! Do not attach any goals to this playtime. Don't expect them to think it's the greatest day of their lives; just expect them to have an OK time that you didn't plan. That is more than enough.

This is the message from the 1950s: their low expectations. Or rather, their reasonable expectations. We demand so much more of our family life—our family *experience*—than previous generations did. And it saddles all of us with an unachievable burden. If you're looking for the main difference between childhood in the 1950s and now, it is that children were freer then. Free to imagine, free to be bored, free to fail, free to be average.

I went back to the 1950s not to be a better parent but to try to enjoy parenting more. I just wanted a better quality of life, and I got it by letting go of rigid ideas about what kids must be doing and allowing things to be simple. If your kids are whiny or combative, they could be craving some independence. If you're sick of hovering, planning, controlling, and worrying, maybe you need a simpler time, too.

Go for it! You only have a few years before they become teens, and then they will not want to play anymore. While they're still young, before they've hit thirteen, is your chance. You can't rearrange your whole life, but you can clear the schedule for a few hours a week of free play: an afternoon after school or perhaps a chunk of time on the weekend.

As moms, we know how to plan fun day trips; we know how to have an exciting birthday party; we know all too well how to have a special time. But we have forgotten how to have an ordinary time. Going back to a simpler time does not mean a lovely picnic in a field with homemade sandwiches and Frisbee tournaments. It means clearing space in a regular day and then allowing the child to fill it. No planning, no guidance, no judgment from you about what they choose to play.

The kids may complain that they're bored; they may beg for their phones or video games. Or they may be shockingly happy doing "nothing," and you will worry that there is something wrong with them, as I did with my kids. You may get a surprising feeling of lightness and joy at how a day that holds so little can feel so full. Let me assure you—it feels great to get out of the rat race. It is not easy, but you don't have to stress out; you don't have to keep up. You don't have to rush to get to someplace wonderful; you're already there.

references

Cantus, Holly. *The Pocket Book of Household Hints*. New York: Permabooks, 1959.

Friedan, Betty. *The Feminine Mystique*. New York: W.W. Norton & Company, 1963.

George, Jean Craighead. *My Side of the Mountain*. New York: Dutton, 1959.

Halberstam, David. *The Fifties*. New York: Villard Books, 1993.

Juster, Norton. *The Phantom Tollbooth*. New York: Random House, 1961.

Marano, Hara Estroff. *A Nation of Wimps: The High Cost of Invasive Parenting*. New York: Crown Publishing Group, 2008.

Wilson, Sloan. *The Man in the Grey Flannel Suit*. New York: Simon and Schuster, 1955.

additional selected reading

Shapiro, Laura. 2004. *Something From the Oven, Reinventing Dinner in the 1950s.* New York: Viking.

Miller, Douglas T. and Nowak, Marion. 1975. *The Fifties, The Way They Really Were.* New York: Doubleday.

Linn, Susan. 2004. *Consuming Kids, The Hostile Takeover of Childhood.* New York: New Press.

Linn, Susan. 2004. *The Case for Make Believe, Saving Play in a Commercialized World.* New York: New Press

Crain, William. 2003. *Reclaiming Childhood.* New York: Henry Holt & Company, LLC

Time Life Books. 1998. *The American Dream: the 50s.* Alexandria, VA: Time-Life Books.

good old-fashioned reads for your children

Morey, Walt. 1965. *Gentle Ben.*

Clark, Pauline. 1964. *The Return of the Twelves.*

Sewell, Anna. 1877. *Black Beauty.*

Wilder, Laura Ingalls. *Little House on the Prairie.* (Series).

Blume, Judy. *Tales of a Fourth Grade Nothing.* (Fudge book series).

London, Jack. 1903. *Call of the Wild.*

McCloskey, Robert. 1943. *Homer Price.*

Alcott, Louisa May. 1880. *Little Women.*

Farley, Walter. 1941. *The Black Stallion.*

Lewis, C.S. 1950. *The Chronicles of Narnia* (Series).

Brink, Carol Ryrie. 1935. *Caddie Woodlawn.*

Montgomery, Lucy Maud. 1908. *Anne of Green Gables.*

Wyss, Johann David. 1812. *The Swiss Family Robinson.*

acknowledgments

Although my 1950s summer seemed to fly by, this book took a long time to come to fruition, and there are several people to whom I am deeply grateful. First, Susan Schulman, who gave me considerable help in revising this book and then found it the perfect home at Familius. I am grateful to be working with Christopher Robbins and the warm and wonderful team at Familius, including Brooke Jorden for her beautiful design and David Miles for his winsome cover. Immense thanks to Michele Robbins, whose patience, insight, and humor helped to shape the book into the best it could be and who made the editing process a delight.

I am indebted to two good friends, C. K. Steefel and Jeanann Zaccaro, for reading early drafts and to Amy Chua, Brigid Schulte, and Monica Holloway for their support. Many thanks to my friend, Jane Daly, for the witty and offhand comment that inspired me to have a 1950s summer and to Mr. Hollister Cantus for generously sharing his mother's book with me and my readers.

Most of all, loving thanks to my family for allowing me to share our stories.

about the author

pam lobley started her career as a comedic actress and performed her material in clubs and theaters all over New York City. She has written several plays, and her humor columns have appeared in many newspapers and online. She is the author of two other books: *Better Living Through Chaos* and *You Definitely Know You're a Mom When . . .* (coauthored with C. K. Steefel). Visit her website at www.pamlobley.com.

about familius

Welcome to a place where parents are celebrated, not compared. Where heart is at the center of our families, and family at the center of our homes. Where boo-boos are still kissed, cake beaters are still licked, and mistakes are still okay. Welcome to a place where books—and family—are beautiful. Familius: a book publisher dedicated to helping families be happy.

Visit Our Website: www.familius.com

Our website is a different kind of place. Get inspired, read articles, discover books, watch videos, connect with our family experts, download books and apps and audiobooks, and along the way, discover how values and happy family life go together.

Join Our Family

There are lots of ways to connect with us! Subscribe to our newsletters at www.familius.com to receive uplifting daily inspiration, essays from our Pater Familius, a free ebook every month, and the first word on special discounts and Familius news.

Become an Expert

Familius authors and other established writers interested in helping families be happy are invited to join our family and contribute online content. If you have something important to say on the family, join our expert community by applying at:

www.familius.com/apply-to-become-a-familius-expert

Get Bulk Discounts

If you feel a few friends and family might benefit from what you've read, let us know and we'll be happy to provide you with quantity discounts. Simply email us at orders@familius.com.

Website: www.familius.com

Facebook: www.facebook.com/paterfamilius

Twitter: @familiustalk, @paterfamilius1

Pinterest: www.pinterest.com/familius

The most important work

you ever do will be within

the walls of your own home.

CPSIA information can be obtained
at www.ICGtesting.com
Printed in the USA
JSHW021513040623
42621JS00003B/19